365 SM

from Buddha

To my darling Loulou.
Happy Christmas,
All my Love,
Pablo
x

365 smiles
from Buddha

robert allen

MQP

introduction

This book is about Buddhism, not as it is found in religious books, but as it is lived. Much of it concerns Thailand, a country where tolerance, kindness, and good humor abound. In particular, it is about the lighter moments of religion because life is too important to be taken seriously.

Some of what follows is autobiographical. The stories are set in Scotland, where I grew up, in Thailand, where I lived for far too short a time, and in England, where I live now. If I'd tried to get all that into one book it would have been as long and involved as one of those classic Russian novels, so I simplified. As Huck Finn said of Mark Twain, "He told the truth, mainly. There's some things which he stretched, but mainly he told the truth." So did I.

I am always grateful for the good karma that introduced

me to some remarkable people. In particular I should mention my good friend Lek and her family, in whose house I lived happily during my time in Thailand. Sean, the Irish monk is, believe it or not, a character who had his origins in two Irish monks. I'd like to thank James and celebrate with him the way in which Buddhism finally sneaked round, over, and under his mental block. I'd also like to send fond greetings to Yukiko. Japanese men say she has become too westernized for their taste. The loss is entirely theirs for she is a remarkable lady of great character and charm.

Names and locations have been changed to protect the privacy of my long-suffering friends. Any vagueness about details of who, where, and when is purely intentional. Those who were there will know the inside story, others won't care.

the flower sermon

Buddha's disciples asked him to preach a sermon.
Instead of talking, he took a lotus blossom and
held it out for them to see. For a long time no one
said anything. Then Maha Kashyapa smiled.
That was the beginning of Zen.

2

bare cheek

The Tibetan holy man Milarepa withdrew to a cave to meditate. He was so indifferent to material comforts that he ate nothing but nettle soup and wore no clothes at all. His sister came to visit him and brought him clothes, but he refused to wear them. "At least for decency's sake," she protested, "take a small piece of cloth and cover your thingummy." Milarepa took the cloth, formed it into a cone and stuck it on his nose.

3

flea fury

In the eyebrows of a certain flea live two
armies of tiny creatures. Constantly they make
war on each other to decide which of them
will rule the universe.

CHINESE STORY

4

a time to die

The young attendant of a Zen teacher broke his master's favorite cup, a valuable antique. At that moment the master returned so the boy hid the pieces behind his back. "Master," he asked, "does everyone have to die?" "Of course, that is natural. We all have only so long to live." The boy produced the broken shards of the cup. "Master, it was your cup's time to die."

5

heart's desire

To an ass a thistle is a delicious treat. The ass sees the thistle. He longs for the thistle. He strains to reach the thistle. At last he breaks free and eats the thistle! He remains an ass.

6

the wise fool

A man who knows he is a fool is not a great fool.

CHUANG-TZU

7

deep water

Some pupils from the Thai girls' school where I taught took me to see the miraculous floating nun. The ancient nun slipped into the pool as easily as a fish. She swam to the center, sat upright in the water, assumed the full lotus position, and then dipped forward until she lay face down in the water. When everyone was quite sure that she must have drowned, she sat up and calmly swam back to the side. She spotted a foreigner in the crowd and got someone to bring me a long bamboo pole. "Measure how deep the water is," urged the nun. I did so; it was about thirteen feet. Everyone gasped in amazement. We lined up to receive the nun's blessing. "What difference does the depth of the water make?" I asked. "Oh, none at all," she assured me, "but people are always impressed by it."

8

the secret of the buddhas

No man has had more images made in his memory than Buddha. There are Thai Buddhas, Japanese Buddhas, Chinese Buddhas, Korean Buddhas, Tibetan Buddhas, and many more. They are very different except for this —nearly all Buddhas smile.

learning to smile

Our mother's smile is the first expression we
respond to and the first one we learn for ourselves.

10

beginner's luck

I was taking a group of beginners through their first session of Zen meditation. It's always quite interesting to see how people react. There were the usual sleepers and the inevitable man with an itch. Someone rather shamefacedly got up and tiptoed out to the restroom. Then there was a girl whose performance held me spellbound. She tossed and turned. Threw her long black hair back and forth, gasping and sighing all the time. A soul in torment would have made less fuss.

When it was over I encouraged them to talk about the experience. Some people had already decided that it was not for them; others were determined to persevere. But the girl who had made all the fuss amazed me. It was, she said, just what she'd hoped. She'd certainly be back for the next session.

11

fragrance

The scent of flowers does not travel against the wind;
but the fragrance of good people travels even against
the wind.

DHAMAPADA

12
the other side

A young monk had been away from his monastery. When he returned he found that a flood had washed out the bridge and the river was too high to ford. Just then he caught sight of his master walking on the far bank. "Master!" he cried, "How do I get to the other side?" The master paused for a moment and yelled back, "Fool! You're already on the other side!"

13

looking-glass buddha

Look in a mirror. What you see is the face of Buddha. Doesn't that make you smile?

14

giving

We must not only give what we have; we must also give what we are.

CARDINAL MERCIER

15

normal discouragement

We sat in a comfortable study in a Cambridge college. There was a roaring log fire and we were listening to a talk by a Tibetan lama. As he talked he constantly fingered his prayer beads. "You know," he said, nodding at the beads, "I've been doing this since I was a tiny child. Sometimes I get really fed up with it. In fact, sometimes I'd like to do this." And he threw the beads into the fire. We all gasped. Then, just at the last split second, he caught the tassel and retrieved the beads. "It's quite all right to be discouraged sometimes," he said with a smile. "We all get discouraged."

meat pie

A man had bought meat at the market and was intending to get his wife to make a pie. On his way home he was confronted by a hungry tiger. In his fright he dropped the meat and the tiger made off with it. "Fool!" shouted the man, "You've got the meat but my wife has the recipe."

17

the right recipe

Many Thais are really thinly disguised Chinese. People call them New Thais. One day we were sitting with some friends discussing the differences between Thai and Chinese Buddhism.

"Of course," said one of the Chinese, "that's all just detail. The real difference between Chinese and Thais is much simpler."

"Really?" I asked, "What is it?"

"When Thai people see something new they think 'Can I eat it?' but when Chinese see something new they think, 'What is the recipe?' They know you can eat *anything* if you only have the right recipe."

18

wrong way

Lei Tan, my Chinese teacher, was describing a famous academic she knew quite well. "He's very sincere and well-intentioned but sometimes he just doesn't get it. Right now he's working hard to study Zen. He gets up early, meditates, reads books, looks up references. And he keeps asking whether his understanding is correct." She sighed. "He doesn't understand that knowing about Zen is quite the opposite to knowing Zen itself. The poor man is exhausting himself running up the 'down' escalator."

buddhists are not brides

My mother received the news that I'd joined the Cambridge University Buddhist Society with a typically pithy maternal remark. "You won't meet a nice girl like that!" Are nice girls not Buddhists, I wondered, or perhaps are Buddhist girls not nice?

20

the use of fear

The parents of a certain boy were so disturbed by his bad behavior that they did not know quite what to do. At last they heard of a Zen master renowned for his strictness. They took the boy along and the father said, "Our son is so unruly we want you to frighten him so that he'll behave." With that the Zen master assumed a dreadful face and let out the kwatz, a loud cry for which Zen masters are famed. The boy nearly jumped out of his skin but his father and mother fainted dead away with fright. When they had all recovered the parents reproached the Zen master.

"You were supposed to frighten our son, not us," they complained. "That's the trouble with fear," replied the master, "once you let it loose there's no stopping it."

precepts

Sean was an Irish monk I met in Thailand. He studied at the monastery near our house and one day came up with this alternative version of a famous story.

"A man who had spent his whole life being particular about keeping the precepts decided to find out what it was like to break one. He thought about it and decided that taking a drink of alcohol would probably be the safest experiment. So he had a glass of wine and enjoyed it so much he had another and another. Eventually he was so drunk that he sat gazing at the moon grinning to himself. "Damn!" he thought, "I can't even remember what the other precepts were."

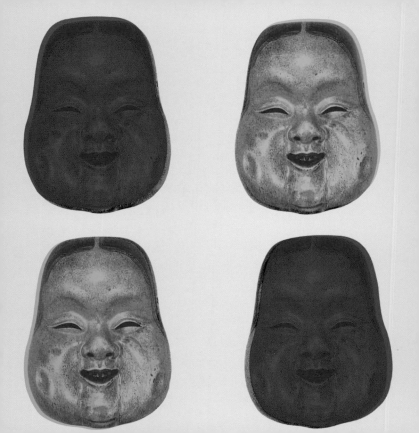

22

the fool and the tigers

A busybody spotted the village fool sprinkling rice around his house. "What are you doing that for?" he asked. "To keep the tigers away," replied the fool. "But there are no tigers around here!" objected the busybody. "I know. Works well, doesn't it?"

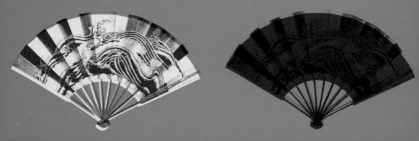

23
what to learn

"Master," asked the new student,
"what will I learn during my zazen?"
"How should I know?" replied the master.
"That's your problem."

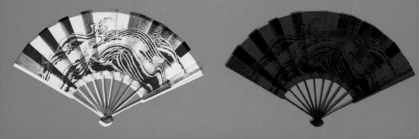

the devil's work

A man sat in the marketplace trying to sell a devil. "It's a good worker," he told people encouragingly, but he got no takers. At last a young farmer showed interest and even offered to pay the full asking price. "Look," said the vendor, "since you've been so generous, I'll tell you the truth. He works well but he'll always be a devil at heart. Just make sure you keep him busy." The farmer took the devil home and, sure enough, he worked well. But one day the farmer went to market and forgot to give the devil any orders. He rushed home and, to his delight, smelled the evening meal cooking as he arrived. "Ah, that's all right he thought." Then he found the devil busy roasting his neighbor's best cow on a spit.

TRADITIONAL JAPANESE STORY

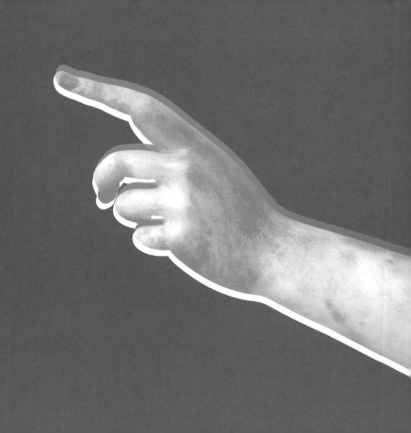

25

less guilt

The Cambridge Buddhist Society meeting was discussing how difficult it was to be vegetarian. One of the group asked the Lama, "Would it be okay to eat small creatures like shrimp, for example?" The Lama laughed, "No, if you really must eat other creatures you should eat elephants. You get a lot of meals from only one elephant. You'd have to sacrifice many, many shrimps to get such a big meal."

26

toothless grin

"Master," asked the pupil,
"how can you say that what
is soft and weak overcomes
what is hard and strong?"
"How many teeth have I?"
asked the Master, showing
a toothless grin.
"None. They are all gone,"
reported the pupil.
"How about the tongue?"
"That's still there."
"And the lips?"
"Yes, of course they're still there."
"Now do you see?"

let the dead bury the dead

Lek and I joined a party of friends on a trip to an island in the Gulf of Thailand. A group of us were standing around in the shallows getting acquainted when a young man who had wandered off alone took a step too far and plunged into deep water. Several people tried to save him but they were not quick enough and he drowned. When we got the body back to shore we discovered that the lad was a stowaway and that everyone had thought he had been brought along by someone else. Funerals have to be held quickly because of the heat but, even after the police made enquiries, no one could discover who the lad had been.

"Oh, well," said Lek, "at least he had no relatives."

"What about the boy himself?" I objected. "He's the one who's dead."

"Yes, but it's the relatives who suffer at funerals. Dead people have better things to do."

28

the fruits of study

"I have read dozens of books about Buddhism,"
announced the young man proudly, indicating his heavily
laden shelves. "What can I do to learn even more?"
"Do you really want to learn Buddhism, or do you just want
to know a lot about it?" asked his friend.
"I want to become enlightened."
"In that case," laughed his friend, "you'd better chuck all
those books away now. It's okay to know about Buddhism
but it's far more important to DO Buddhism."

natural pleasures

If you wish to know the Divine, feel the wind on
your face and the warm sun on your hand.

BUDDHA

good dog

A dog is not considered a
good dog because it is a good
barker. A man is not a good man
just because he's a good talker.

CHUANG-TZU

31
car hell

A monk offered us a tour of the Heaven and Hell
Caves near Bangkok. It was a long, hard climb. The
caves at the bottom were supposed to represent hell
and, as you mounted the tricky route to the summit,
the twisted rocks were supposed to look like
Buddhas. Eventually we arrived breathlessly at the
summit and sighed with relief. "Unfortunately," grinned
the monk, "your car remains in hell, and if you want it
back, you'll have to return there."

a ticklish situation

Our cat, a young and inexperienced hunter, wandered in holding a small but nevertheless poisonous snake coiled in its jaws. The cat wanted to eat the snake and the snake wanted to bite the cat. I had a problem. If I attempted to come between them then, in the manner of domestic disputes the world over, I'd be in trouble with both parties. On the other hand I couldn't just leave them to kill each other. What to do? It was almost a koan. The answer? "Hah!!!" I yelled at the top of my lungs. The cat jumped and released the snake, which lost no time in wriggling back into the garden. I laughed with relief.

33

love the world

See the world as your self. Have faith in the way
things are. Love the world as your self; then you can
care for all things.

TAO TE CHING

good times

Every day is a good day.

ZEN SAYING

35

smoking pleasure

I was about seven or eight. Most adults smoked in those days. I came across a pack of my mother's cigarettes and thought I'd be really helpful by putting them in her cigarette case. Later that day she found the unexpectedly full case and was delighted.

"Look!" she laughed to my aunts, "I had all these cigarettes I didn't know I'd got."

"That was me, Mommy," I said proudly, "I put them in there for you."

"Oh you little devil! They're all crushed."

Everyone laughed. It's funny how free cigarettes are good, but damaged ones bad.

an unexpected smile

I'd just left home for university, hadn't yet made friends, and was homesick. An Irish band was playing in the Student Union so I took myself to the concert and watched, feeling miserable and depressed all the time. I must have looked terrible. Suddenly the lead singer caught my eye and gave me an enormous smile and a wink. That smile is now over thirty years old but I still have it.

unsmiling buddhas

The Spanish are not a smiley people. They're not miserable or unfriendly, they just don't see the point of smiling about nothing. We visited Barcelona and, because it's a large city, got lost frequently. Every time it happened one of the locals would descend on us, take charge of our map, and explain exactly where we needed to go. During a two-day visit it must have happened half a dozen times. You don't have to smile to be a Buddha.

38
the storm

A ship from China to Japan ran into a storm and was tossed about on waves like mountains. One of the crew became hysterical with fear. A Zen master traveling as a passenger told the other crew members to tie a rope to one of the man's ankles and throw him over the side. After a couple of minutes he ordered him to be pulled back on board. Although he lay shivering on deck he was now quite calm.

39
the truth

"What is truth?" a disciple asked.
"Something I have never told," answered the
master, "and I don't intend to start now."

40
the door

All teachers do is show you the door.
The entering is up to you.

CHINESE PROVERB

blessing a car

Lek's husband, Pi Jim, bought a car. It was very smart but secondhand, so he decided to have it blessed by the monks just in case it was contaminated with any evil influences. A couple of monks came and performed a simple ceremony involving smearing little bits of gold leaf on various parts of the car. Pi Jim was very pleased. They were just about to leave when one of the monks asked him to run the engine, which he did.

"The blessing is all very well," said the monk, "but I know a bit about cars. You need new plugs and points as well."

42
unenlightened

A blind man was in the habit of carrying a lamp when he went out at night so that others would not blunder into him. Once, as he made his way along the streets, he ran straight into someone coming the other way.
"What's the matter, didn't you see my lamp?"
"Sorry, but the lamp has gone out."

43

the mulberry leaf

A craftsman carved a jade mulberry leaf for his prince.
It took him three years and was indistinguishable from
the real thing. He was rewarded for his skill with a
pension. When Lieh-tzu heard of this he said: "If it
took the Creator three years to make each leaf, there
would be few trees with leaves on them. The Sage
relies not on human skill but on the operation of Tao.

LIEH-TZU

44

no idea

"What is my self?" a young monk asked.

"What would you do with a self?" asked the master.

"Would it be right to say I have no idea?"

"Throw that idea of yours away right now!"

"What idea?"

"You are carrying about the useless idea of no idea.
Throw it out!"

unwise to smile

Our school taught science to young ladies. It had little time for the arts and languages were only taught as an essential adjunct to learning science. One day there was a staff meeting. My grasp of Thai, best described as rudimentary, was not up to following the conversation. I resorted to the foreigner's secret weapon, the idiot grin. Our headmistress, known universally as The Old Lady, said something and looked encouragingly at me. I gave her the grin. "Excellent," she said, "so you can teach Religion. Go and ask the monks, they'll give some booklets. That is the end of the meeting."

46

mara's daughters

Sean told Lek's three young daughters the story about Buddha's last great effort to gain enlightenment. They liked the bit where Mara, the Devil, sent a flood to drown Buddha but Naga, the World Snake, lifted him clear of the flood. But the bit that really impressed them was where Mara's three sexy daughters turned up to try to distract Buddha with their dancing. The daughters are, of course, supposed to stand for Lust but to pre-teens they just seemed like a really cool pop band. Sean went back to the monastery pleased that he'd done a good job of religious education. He'd have been less satisfied if he knew that the girls immediately set about practicing a dance routine designed to get them jobs in Mara's disco.

47

the goose in the bottle

There is a Zen koan in which a goose is trapped in a large bottle. How can you get the goose out without breaking the bottle? One student replied, "There! It's out!" and became enlightened.

mistaken identity

I went with my Thai family to visit a Chinese temple. Instead of saffron robes the monks wore bright orange pyjamas. The Buddhas weren't the sleek athletic ones found in Thai temples but rather jolly fellows who needed a course at Weight Watchers. The clouds of incense were so thick they were like a fragrant version of an old-time London fog. We were received very kindly and one of the monks took time to talk to us about the temple and the Chinese Buddhist community. On the way back in the car my friend's five-year-old daughter, known as Little Monkey, piped up:

"So that's what a Christian temple is like, is it?"

We explained that it was really a Buddhist temple but she was sure we must have been teasing.

crossing barriers

The smile is the international language of goodwill.

50

artful expression

It is no coincidence that the world's most famous painting is the Mona Lisa. How we are fascinated by that smile!

51
fan zen

A master was with two students when he suddenly tossed his fan at one of them.

"What's this?" he demanded.

The student caught the fan and fanned himself with it.

"Not bad," said the master. "What about you?" and he handed the fan to the other student who first scratched his neck with it and then, opening it out, used it as a tray to offer the master a cake.

"Even better!" exclaimed the master.

52

new broom

Sean came from Ireland to become a Buddhist monk. They gave him one of those long names that means something spiritually uplifting but I never felt right about using it. Settling into the monastery was far more difficult than he'd expected. The spiritual training was all he had wanted, but the arrangements for daily living were chaotic. The Thai life is a sort of semi-organized chaos. Being a helpful lad Sean would make regular suggestions to the abbot for ways to improve the running of the monastery. The old man smiled and nodded but nothing got done. Sean became more frustrated and more insistent that things should be improved. One day the abbot stopped him in full flood and said, "Write me a list of all your suggestions." Sean agreed readily. "And then, write at the top of it 'These are my problems.'"

ripples

Good karma
See how the rings
Cover the water

goldfish

I keep goldfish and find it relaxing sometimes just to sit watching them. I noticed something interesting. When two or more fish dive for the same piece of food and only one of them is quick enough to grab it, what do you think happens? Do the unlucky ones start a fight? Try to tear the food from their rival's mouth? Swear? Sulk? No, they just turn away and find something else to eat. Maybe goldfish are all Buddhists.

55

tao

When superior people hear of the Way
They try hard to practise it.
When the middling people hear of the Way
They sometimes keep to it, and sometimes lose it.
When inferior people hear of the Way,
They laugh at it.
If they didn't laugh, it would not be the Way.

TAO TE CHING

the lucky drunk

A drunken man who falls out of a cart may suffer but he does not die. His bones are just like anyone else's but he meets the accident in a different way. He is neither conscious of riding in the cart, nor of falling out. He has no ideas of life or death or fear, so he does not suffer from contact with the outside world. If such security is to be got from wine, how much more is to be got from Spontaneity?

CHUANG-TZU

57

lack of spontaneity

The centipede was happy, quite,
Until a toad in fun
Said, "Pray, which leg goes after which?"
This worked his mind to such a pitch,
He lay distracted in a ditch,
Considering how to run.

58
buddha behavior

The rules for keeping Buddha images are complicated and, let's face it, very silly. The image must be stored above head height and handled with extreme reverence at all times. No wonder the early missionaries thought that Buddhism was a form of idolatry. So I was more than a little surprised when I discovered Ud, our maid, giving my Buddha a rough cleaning with a duster. She saw my expression.
"Oh it won't matter to him," she said, continuing to buff the little fat smiley Chinese fellow energetically, "he's not from around here."

59

daruma

Daruma, the first patriarch of Zen, is one of my favorite characters. He is seen in many guises; sometimes he is the jolly little doll who cannot be knocked over, at others he is the fierce, bearded foreigner who glowers at you like a hungry tiger. Don't be fooled, there's nothing phoney about his fierceness. You'd have to be brave and stupid to believe that. But, if you look at him carefully, you can see in his expression that, like any good teacher, however much he may scold and shout, he is ultimately concerned for your good. For me, if anyone could personify Zen it would be Daruma.

60

peace at last

A student approached Daruma.
"Please help to pacify my mind,"
he pleaded.
"Bring your mind here and I'll pacify it,"
replied the sage.
"But when I seek my mind I can't find it."
"There," retorted Daruma, "I have
pacified your mind!"

61

obeying the rules

Sean, the Irish monk, would often drop in to visit us when his duties at the monastery were finished and our house became a handy refuge from the rigors of monastic life. The girls were fascinated by the strange "pra farang" or European monk. Though he tried hard to do all the right things he looked very unmonkish. Whereas the Thai monks would wrap their saffron robes around them tightly to avoid exposing naked flesh, he let his flap around as though it were a beach robe.

Proper monks would avoid eye contact, especially with women, but Sean talked to them quite naturally laughing and joking as he'd always done. Some people disapproved and thought that Sean was going to be a very bad monk indeed. These criticisms reached the abbot. He smiled and said, "It's true that he might become a bad monk, but somehow I feel that he is finding his way to becoming a very good one."

the future

Speak of tomorrow and the devil laughs.

JAPANESE SAYING

63

tomorrow

There is no tomorrow. Whatever you want to do, you must do it today.

64
ant sense

An ant crawls across the floor completely unaware of
the entomologist examining it through his magnifying
glass. How could the ant know the world of the
scientist? How could its tiny brain encompass all the
wonders of civilization? The scientist, of course,
suffers from no such difficulties.

65

a good turn

A man was on a journey when he saw a river up ahead and decided to let his donkey stop for a drink. Unfortunately the sides were steep and the donkey nearly slipped into the water. Just then some ducks, frightened by the donkey, started up a loud quacking. The donkey was, in turn, so frightened by the ducks that it immediately scrambled back up the bank.

"Ducks," called the man, "you've done me a good turn. Here's something to reward you." With that he flung them all his small change.

sure shot

A young man was very so proud of his Zen archery
that he challenged well-known master to a contest.
The master accepted and let the young man go first.
He placed the first arrow in the bull's-eye, and the
second split the first, and the third split the second.
The master said nothing but beckoned the young man
to follow him. He led him up a mountain until he came
to a perilous peak where a log jutted out into thin air
over a terrible drop. The master walked out onto the
very tip of the log, unslung his bow and shot three
arrows into a far off tree just as the young man had
done, with each arrow splitting its predecessor. The
young man was grasping onto the rocks and looking
at the abyss in horror. The master smiled and left.

do monks have dirty habits?

"Do you realize," asked Sarah at a Buddhist Society meeting, "that most people think meditation is a dirty habit?" There was a ripple of nervous student mirth. Then, one by one, everyone confessed they'd had the same experience.

"I'm sure Sarah's right," said Adam. "If you tell people you meditate they don't say much but you can see what they're thinking."

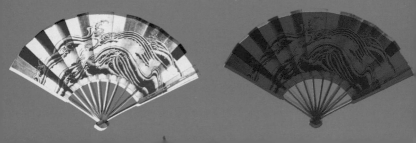

nirvana

It was well-known that when she wanted to build her school the Old Lady went to a firm of builders who tried to cheat her. So she bought out the company and finished the project herself. One day I overheard this conversation between two high school students: "Do you think when she gets to nirvana Buddha will refuse to let her in for being so grouchy?" "Wouldn't do him any good. She'd just build another one next door and put him out of business."

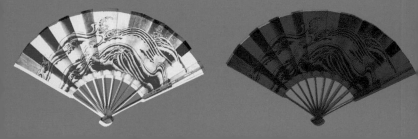

working too hard

A young but earnest Zen student approached his
teacher, and asked the Zen Master:
"If I work very hard and diligently how long will it take
for me to find Zen?"
The Master thought about this, and then replied,
"Ten years." The student then said, "But what if I work
very, very hard. How long then?"
Replied the Master, "Well, twenty years."
"But, if I really, really work at it. How long then?"
asked the student.
"Thirty years," replied the Master.
"But, I don't understand, said the student. "At each time that
I say I will work harder, you say it will take me longer. Why?"
"Because when you have one eye on the goal, you only
have one eye on the path."

70

getting warmer

A traveling Zen master reached a
deserted shrine where he decided to
stay for the night. The weather was
bitterly cold so he took the Buddha
image and used it to make a fire.

reincarnation

A smart young Cambridge student on a backpacking tour turned up at Sean's monastery and drew the Irish monk into a conversation. The student was keen to show off his razor-sharp intellect and mock Sean's Buddhist convictions.

"So," said the student, "if I live an evil life might I be reborn as, say, an animal?"

"Yes, you could," answered Sean.

"How about a ameba? If I was really bad, might I come back as an ameba?"

"Jaysis," came the reply, "have you nothing better to do with your life? You'll find out about reincarnation soon enough I'm thinking."

72
jaysis!

Despite his Buddhist convictions Sean never quite got out of the habit of rolling his eyes heavenwards and sighing, "Jaysis!" at moments of stress. One day the abbot dropped in to see Grandmother, who was a keen supporter of the monastery and had been unwell. We asked how Sean was getting on. The abbot grinned broadly, tried to roll his eyes and said, "Oh, Jaysis!"

the wisdom of a tree

Lao Tzu was traveling with his disciples and they came to a forest where hundreds of woodcutters were cutting the trees. The whole forest had been cut except for one big tree with thousands of branches. It was so big that 10,000 persons could sit in its shade.

Lao Tzu found the woodcutter and asked why the tree had not been cut. He said: "This tree is absolutely useless. You can't make anything out of it because every branch has so many knots in it—nothing is straight. You can't use it as fuel because the smoke is dangerous to the eyes. This tree is absolutely useless, that's why we haven't cut it."

Lao Tzu laughed. He said to his disciples, "Be like this tree.

If you are useful you will be cut and made into furniture. If you are beautiful you will be sold in the market. Be like this tree, absolutely useless, and then you will grow big and vast and thousands of people will find shade under you."

argument

Which is the more powerful argument for
Buddhism, a sermon or a smile?

mrs. greenbaum's visit

The influx of Jewish converts to Buddhism has become so great in recent years that it's led to a whole generation of jokes like this one.

After a journey of thousands of miles Mrs. Greenbaum reached a monastery high in the Himalayas and asked to see the abbot.

"The abbot sees nobody without an appointment and he never sees women," replied the gatekeeper.

"Just tell him Mrs. Greenbaum is here and he'll see me."

"I told you, the abbot never sees women."

"You just tell that Nathan Greenbaum to get his backside out here! His mother's brought him chicken soup."

the warlord

A samurai lord held a whole region by force of arms and terrorized the people. An old Zen master visited him.

"Hold my staff," he said.

"What now?" asked the lord.

"Hold it tight so I can't snatch it back."

The samurai looked amazed. How could an old man snatch a staff from a seasoned soldier?

He gripped the staff tightly.

The master waited, and waited, and waited. Then, when the samurai's arms grew tired and his grip began to weaken, he deftly snatched the staff away.

"There is a limit to what you can achieve by strength alone," he said as he left.

77

go with the flow

The softest aspect of nature is water. It follows the path of least resistance, and is the humblest of all the elements as it always seeks the low point, yet in the end it always overcomes.

ANONYMOUS

choosing a name

Thai names are long and complicated,
which is why everyone hides behind unisex
nicknames like Lek, Noi, Tiew, and the rest.
My friend Lek is really called something
that roughly translates as The Golden
Scales of Justice (her father wanted a boy).
When you take a new baby to the temple
the monks look up a syllable in Pali, the
sacred language of Theravada Buddhism,
and then you embellish on this until you get
the name you want. Then you forget about it.
No one ever uses his or her real name. Though
if in later life you get a run of bad luck, it is
permissible to go back and get a new
one to see if it works any better.

79
tao te ching

I'd been doing some research in the public library when a man approached me wearing a friendly grin.

"Do you recognize me?" he asked.

He looked vaguely familiar, but I couldn't put a name to the face.

"I'm Nick Summers. Thirty years ago we were at school together and you told me to read this." He produced a copy of the Tao Te Ching. "And I did read it. In fact I liked it so much that I still read it, so I just wanted to thank you."

fishy story

A man caught a large fish weighing several pounds. He took it home and told his wife to have it cooked for dinner. She instructed the servants and left them to it. But when they smelled the delicious aroma they were overcome with hunger and ate the whole fish. Then, to try to shift the blame, they made up a story that the cat had rushed into the kitchen, seized the fish, and rushed out. The man found the cat and weighed it. It was the exact weight of the fish.

"If this is the cat," he said, "where is the fish, and if this is the fish, where is the cat?"

the nature of reality

We don't live in the real world.
We live in a world we made up.

FRANK OPPENHEIMER

82

the ox

Oh monks, you must not walk on the Way as the ox is attached to the wheel. His body moves, but his heart is not willing. But when your hearts are in accord with the Way, there is no need of troubling yourselves about your outward demeanor.

BUDDHA

mom the nun

Lek's mother decided that, like a lot of elderly Thai ladies, she would retire to a nunnery. I was astonished. She was a forceful lady and I just didn't see her as a nun. But she went through with it and, after a while, we paid her a visit.

"How are you getting on, Mom?" asked Lek.

"Fine. I like the peace and the meditation, and I've made some friends."

"What about the food? I thought you'd find it hard to give

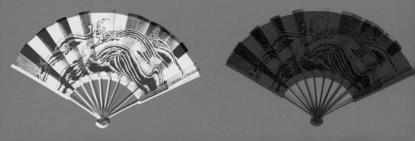

up meat completely."

"No, that's not a problem."

Eventually we took our leave. Just as we left a few whispered words were exchanged and I saw Lek slip something into her mother's hand. As we walked back to the car and I saw Lek grinning to herself.

"What is it?"

"Oh nothing. But it's a good job I thought to bring her some cigarettes, she was dying for a crafty smoke."

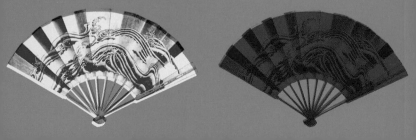

buddha's problem

Sean was fair-skinned and smothered in freckles. Unfortunately the mosquitoes ate him alive. The poor chap was constantly covered in ugly red blotches. He told the abbot about his problem but the only reply he got was, "Don't worry about the mosquitoes, they're Buddha's problem."

"It's all very well to say they're Buddha's problem," Sean complained, "but it's not Buddha who's getting bitten." There was, however, nothing to be done. So he was forced to take the abbot's advice and, ignoring the insects, get on with his work and meditation. Then, to his utter amazement, after six months the trouble stopped. He was, presumably, still being bitten, but his skin no longer erupted in blotches every time it happened.

"Well, would you look at that?" he marveled. "Looks like Buddha took care of it after all."

85

bitten

Zazen,
fat mosquitoes
everywhere

HAIKU BY TAIGI

turtle trouble

We found a turtle wandering around the road outside our house and doing its best to get killed by passing cars. I grabbed it (carefully, because they really know how to bite) and took it to the monastery where the monks had a big pond. I was just dumping the turtle into its new home when Little Monkey piped up: "You'll get merit for doing this." Thais are very keen on merit, the idea that good acts help you to build up a store of credit. I never much liked the idea. It always sounded too much like collecting spiritual Brownie points.

"Oh, you can have the merit if you want it," I said.

Just at that moment Sean arrived.

"You won't get out of it as easily as that," he grinned.

"Giving away your merit to others is especially meritorious."

what if buddha never existed?

There are always people who like to toy with the idea that this or that religious figure did not exist. Was Buddha a real person? Let's suppose for a moment that he wasn't. So what? We have the teaching and it works. There are also countless reliable accounts of enlightenment. The word "Buddha" is, in any case, rarely used in the literal sense. It has many meanings but the idea of an actual man who lived at some specific time is really the least of them.

think about it

Form is emptiness, emptiness is form.
Form is for, emptiness is emptiness.

89

crib sheet

It is said that a book circulates secretly in Japan and changes hands at a high price. It purports to contain the answers to all the best-known koans. Clearly the author had a sense of humor.

90

the land of smiles

An American friend came to visit us in Bangkok. He was
bowled over by the ubiquitous Thai smiles. "I'd heard that
Buddhism was a pessimistic religion all about suffering and
death. What are they all so happy about?"

benefits of buddhism

Sean was talking to me one day about rebirth and whether
we could believe in it. My friend's young daughters came
into the room. Although they were young their English was
excellent and, since they could never quite regard Sean
as a real monk, they had no compunction about joining in
our conversations.

"You're very lucky to be a Buddhist," announced the eldest.

"Why's that?" I asked.

"Because when you die you'll get another go."

"Yes," added Little Monkey, the youngest sister, "Buddhists
can have as many goes as they want."

"What about Christians, Jews and Muslims," enquired
Sean with a grin, "don't they get another go?"

"Oh, no," the girls assured him seriously, "it's the same with
all those other people. When they're dead, they're dead."

92

empty words

Supposing someone was crossing a river by boat and an empty boat collided with it. Even a real grouch wouldn't lose his temper. But if there were someone in the second boat, the occupant of the first would be sure to shout at him. If he didn't take notice then he'd curse and swear. If only we could roam through life empty, who would want to hurt us?

CHUANG-TZU

93

the simple life

Sit. Rest. Work.
Being alone, never weary.
On the edge of the forest, live
joyfully and without desire.
BUDDHA

a man of few words

There is a tale of a strict Buddhist monastery where the monks observed a vow of silence. Each monk was allowed to utter only two words every ten years. After his first ten years one of the monks went to the abbot and was allowed his two words.

"Bed. Hard," he said. Another ten years passed.

"Food. Crap," he said. And another ten years passed.

"I quit!" he yelled.

"I'm not surprised," said the abbot, "you've done nothing but complain since you got here."

the hunter

My father told me that he would go for early morning walks in the country and the rabbits would sit nearby and ignore him. One day he thought it might be a good idea to shoot one or two for the pot. So he borrowed a gun and carried it casually by his side. The rabbits weren't fooled for a moment. Now that he had murder in mind they took fright and ran off before he even had time to take aim.

being yourself

A lady came to ask about meditation and I spent
a long time explaining what it was, how it was done,
and how it helps you to discover your true self.
She listened politely and then said:
"That's all very well, but I'd really rather just be me."

what wat?

There are so many temples, or wats, in Bangkok that it is hard to keep track of them all. Sean joked that we should start a tourist magazine called What Wat? Mistaken identification caused problems. Some friends had been visiting one Buddhist temple after another until they wandered into a Chinese temple where they found some men surrounding a goat. There was a crowd of onlookers. They assumed that they had chanced upon a sort of Buddhist harvest festival. Lek and I arrived a couple of minutes later and, taking in the scene at one glance, realized that this was a fertility rite that had nothing at all to do with Buddhism. Making some excuse about being late we grabbed our friends and hustled them out of the temple in the last few seconds before the goat had its throat cut.

the results of meditation

Ma-tsu sat in meditation when
Huai-jang came and sat beside him.
"Why are you meditating?"
asked Huai-jang.
"To become a Buddha, of course,"
answered Ma-tsu, niggled
at being disturbed.
Huai-jang licked up a tile and started
to polish it with his hand.
"Why are you doing that?" asked Ma-tsu.
"To make a mirror, of course."
"You won't make a mirror like that."
"And you won't become a
Buddha sitting like that!"

99

keep smiling

Enlightenment takes its time to come. Fretting won't help. Remain calm and live joyfully.

100
life and death

Feathered birds, and fishes finned,
And clouds and rain and calm and wind,
And sun and moon and stars declare,
All life is one, everywhere;

That nothing dies to die for good
In clay or dust, in stone or wood,
But only rests awhile to keep
Life's ancient covenant with Sleep.

ELEGY FOR EDWARD THOMAS BY CHARLES SALMON

101

victory

Not even a god can change into defeat the victory of a man who has vanquished himself.

DHAMAPADA

102
choosing your words

There was a multifaith conference and three monks wanted permission to smoke.

"It's just a question of asking the right question," said the Jesuit.

"I'm going to ask my superior if it's possible to smoke while you're praying," said the Dominican.

"That's no good at all," replied the Jesuit.

"The right question is, 'Is it possible to pray while you're smoking?'"

"That wouldn't do for my abbot," said the Zen monk.

"The right question is, 'Is this a cigarette?'"

bad karma

I visited a non-Buddhist friend at the university and somehow we got into an argument about karma. Buddhists believe that good actions bring good results and bad actions bring misfortune. James thought it was all rubbish. We spent quite some time arguing over people who, he insisted, had lived evil but happy and successful lives. Eventually James got annoyed and thumped the desk to reinforce the point he was making. The pile of essays he had been marking fell on the floor and he stooped to retrieve them, overbalanced, and sprawled on the floor himself. As he got up his foot slipped on one of the essays and down he went again. As I helped him to his feet he managed to bump his head on the corner of the desk.

"I suppose," he said bitterly, "that you think you've won the argument, don't you?"

the way to live

Fish are born in water. People are born in the Way.
If fish get ponds to live in they thrive. If people live
according to the Way they live in peace.

CHUANG-TZU

105

royal rage

Two kings were about to go to war over the construction
of a reservoir. Their armies were drawn up facing each
other when Buddha appeared between them and
summoned the kings to him.

"Tell me, is the earth of any intrinsic value?"

"Of no value at all," replied the kings.

"Is the water of any intrinsic value?"

"None at all."

"And the blood of kings, is that of any intrinsic value?"

"It is priceless," they replied.

"And do you really want to risk something priceless
for things of no value?"

The kings decided not to fight after all.

106
women

As Buddha lay on his deathbed his
disciple Ananda asked:
"How are we to conduct ourselves,
Lord, with regard to women?"
"Do not see them, Ananda!"
"But if we should see them what are we to do?"
"Abstain from speech."
"But if they speak to us, Lord, what are we to do?"
"Keep wide awake, Ananda!"
To which Sean added, "Only monks could think
they'd get rid of women easily as that!"

mostly harmless

Most Western Buddhists are strict vegetarians and take the duty of harmlessness very seriously. In the East people are much more relaxed on this point. The family were sitting at dinner one day when I raised the subject. "Well," said Lek's sister-in-law, "it's like this. I didn't kill this chicken, the butcher did. Now if I come across a dead chicken it would be wasteful not to eat it when there are people starving, wouldn't it? So eat up and stop being silly."

108
debating religion

James had a sort of love-hate relationship with Buddhism. While he insisted that he was a card-carrying atheist who despised all religions, he insisted on discussing Buddhist beliefs on every possible occasion. The abbot, who was much traveled and a subtle debater with a wide knowledge of the world, seemed to enjoy James's visits. One day, when they had been at it for some time and James was clearly getting the worst of the argument, he wailed, "If you're going to keep clouding the issue with facts I'm not going to argue with you any more!"

buddhist plants

The abbot would sit in the monastery grounds and give regular talks about Buddhism to anyone who wanted to drop in and listen. One day, just after he'd finished, I mentioned how beautiful the clumps of bamboo in the garden were.

"Of course," he smiled, "bamboo is a good Buddhist plant."

"How do you make that out?"

"Think about how it benefits its fellows. You can build with it, make a million useful things from it, even eat it. Although it is so strong that it is almost impossible to break, it bends to the wind and does not resist by force. Yet all it requires in return is simple sustenance. If only we could all be more like the bamboo!"

110
gasping for truth

A Zen pupil asked his master how he should search for truth. The master seized him by the arm and dragged him to a water tank where he held his head under until the poor boy nearly drowned. When he was hauled out the master said:
"That is how we seek the truth, with the urgency of a man deprived of air seeking breath."

111

missionary zeal

Mary-Beth was an American missionary for a sect so obscure that she may well have been the only member. She had made it her business to convert all the idolatrous Buddhists. She showed up at the monastery regularly where she was received politely, given tea, and encouraged to share her views. She was liked for her genuine good humor, but her knowledge didn't always keep pace with her huge enthusiasm. One day she exclaimed, "If you forsake false gods you will be born again!" Sean, suppressing a grin, muttered, "Are you going to tell her, or shall I?"

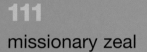

112
deep waters

It was the time of the fall floods and the streams all poured into the river, which swelled to enormous size. Its banks became so far apart that, from one side, it was impossible to tell whether it was a cow or a horse standing on the opposite bank. The Spirit of the River laughed with joy at its own sheer power. Then it arrived at the ocean and gazed in amazement at the vast expanse of water that faced it.

"He who has only heard part of the truth thinks no one is equal to himself. What a fool I am!"

CHUANG-TZU

113

man's great abyss

Heaven and hell are worlds within us.
Man is the great abyss.

HENRI FRÉDÉRIC AMIEL

114

death delayed but not defied

Mary-Beth was very keen to win converts by
telling stories of miracles allegedly performed by
the head of her sect. She was blissfully unaware
that, though most Thai people love stories of the
supernatural, strictly speaking miracles are a major
no-no in Buddhism. One day she told the abbot
how her guru had raised a man from the dead.
He listened attentively and then asked:
"And will this man die eventually?"
"Yes, I suppose so."
"Then surely his problem is not solved,
merely postponed."

are you being funny?

I was going out with a Japanese girl
called Yukiko and took her to some
family celebration or other where she
met my Aunt Jane, a lady of very
traditional views. Jane could never resist
the opportunity to drag her opinions into
every conversation and soon she'd
uncovered the information that Yukiko
was a Buddhist. "But you believe in Jesus
as well, of course," she said confidently.
"Buddhists respect all religions," came
the tactful reply, "but I don't really know
anything about Jesus." Next time I met
Jane she mentioned Yukiko.
"A pretty girl, but what a very
strange sense of humor."

crime and punishment

The Old Lady was not a great believer in modern ways. When we got paid she simply called us one by one to the office and handed out wads of banks notes. Lek and I went to the bank to deposit our salary. As we stood in a short line Lek whispered, "Notice this girl." We were served by a typical middle-class woman in her mid-twenties, pretty, smiling, immaculately turned out. When we were outside Lek said, "Her husband had an affair and she shot him six times. Now she is out on bail but she will go to prison for a long time." Week after week we were served by the same person and each time her smile was unfaltering. Then one day she bowed as we left and said that she was leaving her job. Later she was jailed for twenty years.

117
a speaking silence

Three monks undertook a vow of silence so that they could concentrate on their meditation. After two days one of them suddenly said, "I've kept my vow all this time!" Immediately one of the others said, "Well, you've broken it now." The third replied smugly, "I am the only one who hasn't spoken."

ring of truth

A certain king called together his wise men and commanded them to have a magic ring made for him. It should cheer him up when he was unhappy, but when things were going well it should stop him from getting proud and overbearing. They went away and puzzled over the problem for a long time. At last someone had a bright idea. A gold ring was brought to the king and on it were engraved the words, "This too shall pass."

119

any objections?

An elderly lady entered the Buddhist Society library and approached the desk.

"Do you have anyone here who can answer my objections to Buddhism?" she asked.

Everyone pricked up his or her ears. The librarian was an Austrian lady of notoriously uncertain temper.

"What are your objections?"

"Well, why for instance, did Buddha not speak out against the caste system in India?"

"In fact he did. But he wasn't a politician; he left that to Gandhi. Any more stupid questions?"

To everyone's amazement the lady took out a subscription to the society on the spot.

120

round and round

"What I don't understand,"
said a non-Buddhist friend,
"is why you go on about old
age, sickness, and death."
"Why, don't you think that's
what happens to us?"
"Oh, sure, but since you
keep getting reborn why
don't you talk about birth,
youth, and beauty instead?"

121
who are you?

A Buddhist sage was brought before the emperor of China for an interview. The emperor listed all the good works he had done, the temples he had paid to have built, the numbers of monks he supported. Then he asked, "What is my merit for all this?"

"None at all," replied the sage.

"And who are you to address me like this?"

"I haven't the faintest idea," replied the sage as he left.

the bare bones of wisdom

Chuang-tzu was traveling when he came across a skull. He took it and, settling down for the night, used it as a pillow. In the night the skull appeared to him in a dream and offered to tell him about death.

"In death there is no sovereign above and no subject below. The workings of the four seasons are unknown. Our existences are bounded only by eternity. The happiness of a king is not more than that which we enjoy."

Chuang-tzu asked him if he would not rather be alive again. The skull looked horrified.

"How should I throw away such great happiness and once again become involved in the troubles of humanity?"

123

open house

A Western house serves to divide inside from outside, to protect its inhabitants from the rigors of the weather. In Thai houses the division is merely notional. No matter how hard you try the outside seeps in. Mosquitoes, lizards, spiders, beetles, and even the odd snake are all regular visitors. Visitors also drop in for a meal without prior notice. It's the custom. This difference is reflected in the attitudes of the people. Westerners divide this from that, here from there, black from white. In Thailand it is easy to take a Buddhist view, to see everything as part of one great whole and all creatures as dependent on each other.

The robb'd that smiles steals something from the thief.

OTHELLO, ACT I, SC. III, L. 208

daily bread

Cilantro is a pungent herb much used in Thai cooking. Each day the monks would walk in single file from door to door collecting offerings of food from the neighborhood. They would walk slowly and solemnly keeping their gaze downward and offering a grave bow by way of thanks. Even though we knew them all well, this was not an occasion for chat. The monks are not allowed to express any preference for food; they have to accept what they're given, even if the food has spoiled. One day I looked up from feeding our pet fish to see Sean, as usual bringing up the rear, apparently muttering something urgently to Lek, who waved him away impatiently.

"What was that all about?"

"He'll never learn. He said, 'Thanks for the food, but could please go easy on the cilantro in future?'"

126

insufficient merit

Lek's dad had always had a rather strained relationship with his family. He worked in the timber trade and spent most of his time up country supervising logging camps. These trips also involved cigarettes, whiskey, and wild, wild women in profusion. His family never lacked for money but never got much of his attention. Eventually his health began to fail and, in traditional style, he decided to make some merit ready for his next life. He paid to have a large Buddha statue regilded in gold leaf. Then he died. We went along to a ceremony to celebrate the refurbishment of the statue. During the ceremony Lek saw a huge cockroach crawling around the foot of the Buddha. "Tough luck, Dad," she murmured, "didn't work, did it?" The cockroach, possibly through embarrassment, made no reply.

127

cake

A monk asked Yun-men, "What teaching
goes beyond the Buddhas and patriarchs?"
"Sesame cake," was the reply.
Don't you feel your hair stand on end?
BLUE CLIFF RECORD

making peace with the welsh

My Japanese friends Yukiko and Midoli heard of a Buddhist temple a couple of hours' drive away from Cambridge. They wanted to visit. I'd never heard of it but Yukiko was adamant, so we set out. At first it was an anticlimax. It wasn't a temple, just a peace pagoda, a sort of monument. We sat and ate lunch. Soon another little group joined us. They were Welsh, two girls and a boy, on vacation. We got chatting and it turned out they were Buddhists too. Midoli offered to share our lunch with them (she always made far too much). When they left the boy said:

"I wasn't sure I'd like the English, but you seem okay. I was surprised you were a Buddhist."

"I'm originally really from Scotland," I explained.

"Oh, that explains it." He thought for a moment. "You're still crap at rugby, of course," he added.

Of course.

the sage

The true sage ignores God. He ignores man.
He ignores a beginning. He ignores matter.
He moves in harmony with his generation and
avoids suffering. He just takes things as they
come and is never overwhelmed. How can
we become like him?

CHUANG-TZU

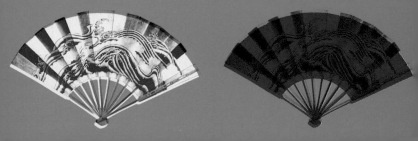

imagine

*"Imagine there's no heaven, it's easy if you try,
No hell below us, above us only sky."*

When John Lennon wrote that he upset a lot of religious people. I don't think he meant it as an atheist anthem; he just had a rather Eastern view of life. Buddhists don't place much emphasis on "religion"; it's all just the way life is. Sometimes we call it "dharma" which means "law". Do you have to believe in the Law of Gravity? No, if you overbalance you fall, believe it or not.

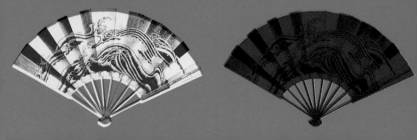

131

the power of nothing

A sage said to his disciple, "You see that tree?"

"Yes, Master."

"Go and fetch me one of the seeds."

The disciple did as he was told.

"Now split it open. What do you see?"

"A little kernel."

"Split it open. What do you see?"

"Some tiny grains."

"Split one open. What do you see?"

"Nothing, Master."

"Yet from that nothing this mighty
tree grew. And you also came
from that nothing."

of bras and buddhism

I was setting out on a trip home when Lek slipped me a list of items—mostly cosmetics and underwear—that she and her friends could not possible live without. I bribed my mother to buy it all and found that Lek's order filled a whole suitcase. On the plane back I chatted to a monk that I knew slightly. At customs in Bangkok an Anglican bishop approached us and struck up a conversation. The line wound slowly forward and eventually it was my turn

"Open the bag," said the official.

And thus it was that two divine gents were astonished to find themselves entering the country in the company of an apparent underwear fetishist.

133

the monk and the tiger

Some moral tales are instructive;
some are plain silly. This one, often
heard in Theravadin circles, used to
reduce us to helpless laughter.
A wandering monk came across
a starving tigress and her cubs.
Rather than let the animals perish he
decided to offer his own body to feed
them. He approached the tigress but
it was too weak from hunger to attack
him. So he drew a knife and cut his
own throat so that the tigers could
feast on his flesh.

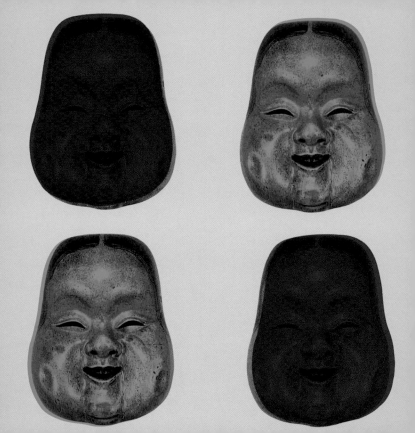

unequal struggle

James was still in the habit of arguing with the abbot as often as possible. It seemed a rather masochistic habit since the old man was a clever and subtle debater and James, in spite of his Cambridge degree, was never able to get one over on his adversary. I asked him one day why he did it. "Well, have you not noticed that he's never content just to win the argument? He always leaves you understanding something you hadn't seen before. I've learned more from him than I did in three years at university."

135

mai ben rai

This is one of the first Thai phrases anyone learns. It's hard to translate. It's not nearly as overtly religious as the Muslim "Inshallah" (As Allah wills it). Some people think it means nothing more than "hey ho" or "whatever," but they're wrong. Mai ben rai expresses an easygoing tolerance that is at the very heart of Buddhism. Buddhist tolerance does not come from its doctrines but from the soil in which they grew. Had Buddhism arrived in the West earlier it would soon have become a nightmare of schism, persecution, and bloodlust. It was saved from that by an attitude so tolerant that it allows people to be members of several religions at the same time without experiencing any feeling of contradiction. It is something we in the West will really enjoy when we finally get the hang of it.

136

religion

A religion is what is left over when
you've forgotten all the important bits.

heaven and hell

A samurai lord visited a Zen master out of curiosity.

"Tell, me," demanded the lord, "are heaven and hell real?"

"I see you're a samurai," said the master. "But you look like a very scruffy and disreputable one to me."

The lord was outraged and went for his sword.

"Oh, you have a sword, do you? I bet it's a blunt old thing that couldn't cut anything."

The lord, apoplectic with rage, raised his sword to strike.

"There open the gates of hell," observed the master calmly.

The samurai, realizing what he was about to do controlled himself and sheathed the sword. The master smiled.

"And there open the gates of heaven," he said.

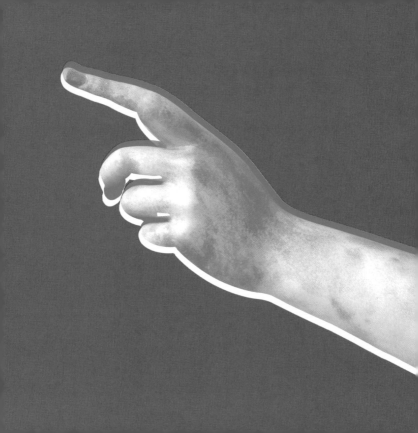

138
just skin deep

Thais sometimes have difficulty with the concept of Western Buddhists. Sean was walking down the lane to our house when a youngster yelled out, "Hey, you!" which is the normal way Thai street kids start conversations with foreigners. Sean was a bit taken aback because monks are always treated with huge respect. Not even a snot-nosed brat would think of addressing one familiarly. The kid continued, "I want to go to America," and then added proudly, "My big sister is a Christian, just like you!" Sean was left pondering the fact that his shaven head and saffron robe were apparently less potent religious symbols than his white skin.

jobbing lama

A lama I knew had a job at a famous London museum
when he wasn't busy teaching Buddhism. One day he
told me how he got it. He had recently arrived in the UK
as a refugee was wandering around the Tibetan section of
the museum partly because he was homesick and also
because he was broke and the museums were free.
A curator passed by, glanced at him and walked on.
As he got down the hall a thought struck him.
He'd seen the lama moving his lips!
He dashed back.
"Were you reading that?" he asked excitedly.
"Oh, yes," replied the lama.
"But it's an ancient script. No one knows how to read it."
"I do. Look I'll show you."
Five minutes later he was offered a job.

table manners

I was trying to interest the lama
in a literary project I was working
on. I invited him to lunch and
picked out a suitable restaurant
with a vegetarian menu. As we
arrived I stood back to guide
him through the door first.
"Oh no," he said, gently but
firmly propelling me through
the door, "you go first.
This is my custom."

as the tree bends, so it falls

A Buddhist layman was dying. He had not yet
attained enlightenment and was worried about
his next rebirth. A monk came to visit him and
he confided his problem.

"Have you lived a good or a bad life?"
asked the monk.

"I've tried very hard to do good, though I
haven't always succeeded."

"When a tree is cut down does it fall the way
the tree bends or the other way," asked the monk.

"The way it bends, of course."

"Then don't worry," smiled the monk,
"you will also fall the way you are inclined."

142

dhana

Buddhism places great emphasis on dhana or giving. This is not the same as what we call charity, it covers a much wider spectrum, as I discovered. Teaching in Bangkok is hot work. When I showed signs of melting one of my students would put her hand up and ask if I'd like a drink. She'd then slip out of the classroom only to reappear moments later with an iced Coke. I assumed that they were going to the staff room where a supply of Coke was kept for the teachers. It was only later that Lek told me the girls had drawn up a roster for this duty and they bought the drinks from their allowance money.

143

seeing the light

It's much easier to believe in
God on sunshiny days.

LORD BYRON

144

rhinoceros

The abbot was fond of a poem with the refrain, "Wander lonely as rhinoceros." The idea was that, if you can't find companions who are serious enough to accompany you on your spiritual journey, you should be prepared to go it alone rather than compromise your beliefs. How such a poem ever got to Thailand, where the rhinoceros is unknown, is hard to imagine. One day, when we'd heard this umpteen times, Sean whispered, "I've never had the heart to tell him the ruddy things live in herds!"

sleepy meditator

A young lady called Tiew came to one of the monastery discussions and monopolized the conversation by talking endlessly about the wonders of meditation.

"Do you know," she gushed, "I flew from Bangkok to Hong Kong and meditated so hard that I hardly noticed the length of the journey."

"Yes," replied the abbot, "I always sleep on planes as well."

meritorious conduct?

A man's wife died and he hired a monk to say prayers for her soul.

"Will these prayers help my wife?" he asked.

"Not only your wife but all sentient beings."

"But my wife is not very strong and all those other beings will take advantage of her and grab her merit. Can't you say prayers just for her?"

"We Buddhists believe that we must strive for the good of all beings."

"Yes, that is a good teaching. But my neighbor is grouchy and disagreeable to me. Couldn't you just leave him out of all those sentient beings?"

147

the chinese monk

All sorts of people end up in a Buddhist monastery. In ours
there was a Chinese monk who not only spoke very little
Thai but also seemed to be a bit simple. People treated
him kindly but in a slightly patronizing way.
"Watch that monk carefully," said the abbot, "and he'll
teach you something valuable."
So I did. At first I couldn't see what it was but then, at last,
it dawned on me. Whatever needed doing, the little Chinese
monk did it. He never quarreled about whether it was his
turn. He never expected thanks or praise for what he did,
he just got on with it. If people thought him unimportant he
appeared not to notice. Of all the monks in the monastery
he was probably the one who was closest to the ideal.

148

the lucky man

A man found a wild horse and captured it. His neighbors told him how lucky he was. Perhaps, he replied. His son tried to ride the horse and was thrown and broke a leg. How unfortunate, said the neighbors. Perhaps, answered the man. Soldiers came to conscript young men for the army but, of course, they didn't take the boy with the broken leg. How lucky, cried the neighbors. Perhaps, replied the lad's father.

149

well, well, well

There was once a well that provided water for the farmers as they worked in the fields. They called it "Our Wonderful Well." One day a man was found drowned in it. From then on they were scared and referred to it as "That Terrible Well". Later it turned out that the drowned man was a criminal who had been fleeing justice. Suddenly the well acquired a new name, now it was the "Well of Justice."

stairway to heaven

When a monk dies he is cremated and a "stupa," shaped rather like an inverted ice-cream cone, is built over his ashes. Usually they are quite small, but the one for the founder of our monastery was huge and had a stairway going up the outside to a little shrine at the top. Sean was often seen going up there and was much praised for his devotion to the memory of the founder. I wondered why, so I asked him.

"The founder? Oh, I hadn't thought about who was under it, I just like the exercise."

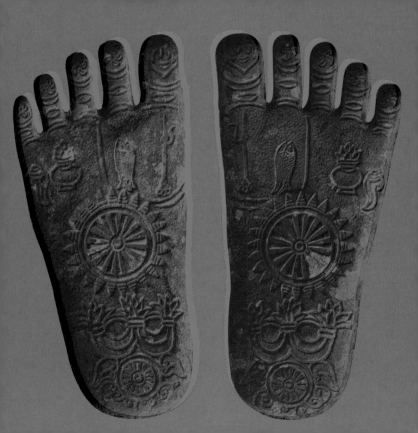

whose religion is it anyway?

Like all religions Buddhism has picked up a mass
of customs and superstitions that were not there
in the early days. The growing Western interest in
Buddhism leads to some interesting arguments and
misunderstandings. The more tactless Westerners
like to point out that these customs are not only not
"real" Buddhism but some of them (like fortune-telling,
magical amulets, and so on) are quite heretical.
Buddha was quite specific about avoiding
superstition. To which the locals retort with
some feeling, "Whose religion is this anyway?"

jasmine

Sean accused me of having a "Protestant nose" just because incense smoke made me cough. But I love the smell of jasmine. Kids would haunt the traffic jams selling strings of flower heads cunningly stitched together. The more jasmine they contained the more you'd pay. Sometimes we used them to freshen the car but often we took them to the temple as an offering. I know that nirvana is beyond the range of the senses but I can't quite suppress a secret hope that it will smell of jasmine.

153

black-nosed buddha

A certain Zen nun had her own Buddha
that she took with her on her travels.
She arrived at a temple where she
planned to stay and found a hall full
of Buddhas. She put hers among them
but, so that her offerings of incense
would go only to her own Buddha,
she made a funnel that would direct
the aroma straight to his nose. In time
the Buddha's nose turned black and
he became the ugliest of all the
Buddhas in the hall.

154

birth and death

Birth is not a beginning,
death is not an end.

CHUANG-TZU

155

buddha rocks!

A rock star, who I won't name, had a hefty drug habit. He turned to a Tibetan lama for advice and visited his meditation center in the hope of finding help. As he was driving down from London he realized that he was so high he wasn't safe to drive, so he parked the car and phoned for a taxi. When he arrived he asked if someone would take the taxi to where he'd left the car and bring it back. He assumed that the lama would send an assistant but, in fact, he went himself. The car turned out to be a Porsche, not exactly the sort of vehicle the lama was used to. He found it was like riding a racehorse. Ironically his progress back home was so erratic that he got stopped by the police on suspicion of drunk driving.

the praying mantis

At a Thai meal the ladies sit separately from the men at one long table. By convention they can't hear each other (so that the men can make rude jokes with impunity). Lek's brother, Noy, didn't like Westerners much so one evening he produced a praying mantis and dropped it "as a joke" on my bare arm. The mantis is harmless to people but looks like something from outer space. Noy hoped I'd yell blue murder and brush it off. I looked at the mantis and it looked back at me. Eventually it got fed up and wandered off. Afterward a disappointed Noy told his sister that all that meditation must have really been working. He'd never known the mantis trick to fail before. Lek laughed as she told me. "It's a good job he didn't choose a big hairy spider, isn't it?" she concluded. She knew me much better than her brother.

157

perfection

Western visitors to the monastery would often expect the monks to be perfect, but kindly, enlightened sages. They'd usually watched too many episodes of Kung-Fu on TV. It was comical to see how disappointed they were to see that monks are just human beings with frailties and foibles like the rest of us. People were often deeply shocked to find that many monks are partial to cigarettes! They'd forgotten the saying, "Water that is too pure has no fish."

the way of life

He not busy being born,
Is busy dying.

BOB DYLAN "IT'S ALRIGHT, MA (I'M ONLY BLEEDING)"

159
durian fruit

The abbot was in the habit of likening human desire to craving for the durian fruit. James didn't understand, so we bought him one to try.

"God, that smells vile! I'm not eating any of that."

"Hold your nose and eat just a little."

"It's delicious."

"Exactly. Now you know why the abbot uses it in his talks. People crave it even though it's disgusting. There have even been murders over the ownership of durian trees. What better illustration of the folly of human passions?"

prayer for the john

"They have prayers for everything round here,"
said Sean with feeling. "They even have one
for going to the jacks."
"Really? How does it go?"
"Oh, I have my own. It goes, 'Please, Buddha,
would you ever do something about this diarrhea!'"

holy orders

Knowing that Sean's family were strict Catholics I asked him what they thought about him being a Buddhist monk. "They were pretty cut up at first. But then they had the idea of telling people that I was away studying for the priesthood."

162

the young swordsman

A young man went to live with a master of sword fighting as his pupil. For months all he was allowed to do was help with household chores. At last he plucked up courage and complained that he was learning nothing about sword fighting. Next day, as the lad was sweeping the floor, the master crept up behind him and whacked him with a wooden sword. From that time on the boy had to be constantly on the alert day and night for there was no time when he was safe from the master's sudden attacks.

registration

The teachers all had to sign
in as they arrived at school.
At 9 A.M. Lek would go and
draw a line under the last name
so that any late comers could
be found out and scolded by
the boss, but she'd always
leave a couple of lines' space
under the last entry.
"Doesn't that rather spoil the
point of the exercise?" I asked.
"But maybe they are already
sorry to be late. Why should I
make them sorrier?"

164

cardiac arrest

I was at the Buddhist Society one day when a rather bumptious young man was giving instruction in meditation. He was describing the approved method involving watching your breathing. Then he said, "I used to concentrate on my heartbeat until, one day a monk asked, 'What will you do when your heart stops?'" He seemed very pleased with this piece of profound wisdom handed down from an actual monk. Just then a first-year student piped up, "And what are you going to do when your breathing stops? Or do you think you can still breathe when you're dead?"

the hyena and the fly

A hyena was boasting to the other animals one day.
"I'm not afraid of the lions. In fact I go right up to their
kill and manage to steal bits from under their noses."
A fly happened to be passing. He said:
"Big and fierce as you are you don't dare do what I
do. I walk on their lips and eat my food right out of
their mouths."
"Huh, you only get away with it because you are
too puny for the lions to bother about."
"That may be so," replied the fly, "but the fact
remains, I feast in safety while you skulk like a thief."

Any flea as it is in God is nobler than
the highest of the angels himself.

ECKHART

167
vile bodies

Sean was telling us that one of the exercises monks were expected to undertake was meditating on the disgusting nature of the human body. They were encouraged to think of hair, sweat, snot, and other excretions, and to awaken in themselves a distaste for our physical being. He confessed that he'd found it difficult at first but was now making good progress. "How did you manage that?" I asked. He grinned. "I started to think about your body instead of mine."

hannah and the old lady

The Old Lady's eldest son fell in love with a Swede called Hannah. The Old Lady wasn't against Europeans but foresaw problems with a mixed marriage. So she packed her son off to the monastery where, as was the custom, he would spend a year as a monk. To show she wasn't just being spiteful she gave Hannah a job at the school. When her son finally emerged from his cloistered existence the couple were as fond of each other as ever. The Old Lady shrugged and gave in. She said that if even the monks couldn't extinguish his passion it must be for the best.

time for buddhism

Once a revolutionary socialist
wandered into a university Buddhist
society meeting and began to heckle.
"Your Buddhism is just a bourgeois interest,"
he announced. "Workers and peasants
don't have time for that sort of nonsense."
The monk who'd been invited to lecture smiled.
"You find Buddhists in universities, but you
find millions more bent double in paddy
fields planting rice. Maybe if you met more
of us your opinion would improve."

170
candle

A monk was demonstrating the truth of rebirth by showing how one candle could be used to light another. In this way the flame of life was passed from one birth to another. The abbot happened to be passing. He took the candle, blew it out, and handed it back. "Now do it," he said, and walked away.

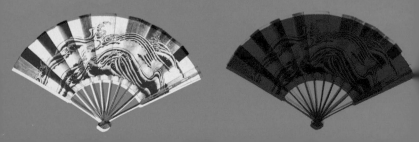

lotus

The lotus is what we'd call a water lily, a beautiful and delicate flower. It's often used as a symbol in Buddhism where it has a number of meanings and appears in all sorts of teaching stories. One of my favorites is this: the bottom of a lotus pond is a filthy mass of stinking slime, yet it produces such wonderful flowers. Do not despise the "dirty" side of life, let it act as fertilizer for your flower.

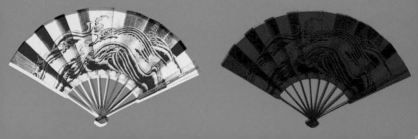

the young stalinists

I once heard some old Russians talking of their young days as enthusiastic supporters of the revolution. They had labored tirelessly to build a power station. The food was poor, the accommodation was basic, and they worked long hours yet they remembered it as the happiest time of their lives. Political prisoners were detained in a labor camp nearby. Their conditions were not much different to those of the young revolutionaries, yet the prisoners sickened and died. Even when the young communists found out about Stalin's black side, they could never get over the great elation they had felt in the early days. If belief in something as mundane as communism could produce such results it's small wonder that people still find religion important in their life.

a fishy tale

A group of monks came together for a meal. Someone, knowing that they were all strictly vegetarian, decided to play a joke on them by adding fish to one of the main dishes. Most of them realized in time and avoided the dish, but an elderly Zen master cleared his plate with relish.

"That was fish!" one of the monks objected. "You shouldn't eat the flesh of another sentient being."

The master fixed his critic with a stern gaze.

"And how do you know that was fish?" he asked pointedly.

the best test

"It is the test of a good religion
whether you can joke about it."

G.K. CHESTERTON

what sort of snake?

The Pasteur Institute in Bangkok breeds snakes so that their venom can be turned into serum. It also treats victims. People treat it as a zoo and go to watch the snakes. I often took Lek's kids there. One day an old peasant woman came in with her foot blown up like a football. The doctor asked her a question and obviously got a dusty answer, but I didn't understand her dialect and asked the kids for a translation. "The doctor asked her what sort of snake bit her," offered Little Monkey, "and she said, 'Who knows? Do you think the snake is sitting around wondering what sort of old woman it bit?'"

176

lucky writing

A famous calligrapher was commissioned to
produce a piece for a wealthy man. He wrote:
"Grandfather dies, father dies, son dies."
His patron was outraged.
"How dare you pollute my house with such
an ill-omened piece of work!"
"On the contrary, what I have written is the
normal course of nature and therefore most
fortunate. Think what a disaster it would be if
things turned out otherwise."

177
practice

Buddhists usually speak of "practice" rather than "meditation." James had a poster of the Great Buddha of Kamakura in his room. Under it he had written, "Does practice make perfect?"

A blue sky is neither blue nor sky.

james and the tibetans

For some odd reason the British seem to have a particular attraction to Tibetan Buddhism. Even James found it getting round, over and under his mental block. He read up on it extensively and spent much time investigating the differences between the Tibetan and Theravada schools. He'd then plague everybody for explanations. One day the abbot said, "The differences are not important. Sugar tastes the same whether you eat the raw cane or put the granules in your coffee. Concentrate on the essentials and you will see that, while they differ in form, they are at heart the same."

the leper

In the Chinese state of Wei lived a leper called Ai T'ai To. Those who lived with him liked him and made no effort to drive him away. He never preached to people, but put himself into sympathy with them. He had no power to protect people nor did he have any favors to bestow. His disease made him hideously ugly but, even so, people were attracted by the greatness of character and the depth of his understanding.

The Duke of Ai sent for him and was so impressed that he made him prime minister. However, the leper, a man of simple tastes, could not adapt to the life at court and soon left. The Duke was as upset as if he had lost a close friend.

CHUANG-TZU

181

everyday miracles

There is nothing quite as funny, or as downright miraculous, as everyday life. Think about it. Think about time, for example. Where does it come from? Where does it go? If you think long enough you will see that there is nothing "ordinary" or "everyday" about it. As the writer Mervyn Peake said, "To be born at all is miracle enough."

182

garee

There is an Indian-style curry that the Thais call garee. Grandmother had a vegetarian batch made up for the monks and Sean immediately developed a taste for it. He wasn't quite sure why every time he said he enjoyed a nice garee, the other monks grinned. Eventually we told him. Said in the wrong tone it is a slang word for prostitute.

183

everything takes time

A samurai was invited to lunch by a Zen master. The master cooked the meal himself and it was taking a long time. Occasionally he would reappear and assure his guest that the food was coming, but nothing happened. Samurai were important people who were used to deferential treatment. Eventually the nobleman was hopping mad. Then, just as his temper was about to overflow, the Zen master appeared with the food. They ate and the samurai, who had calmed down by now, complimented his host on the meal.

"Thank you," replied the host, "all it takes is time."

184

stealing the sword

My Chinese teacher once got me to translate this from classical Chinese. Once a man had his sword stolen and immediately suspected a neighbor of the offence. Everything about the man announced his guilt. He walked like a thief, talked like a thief, ate like a thief, drank like a thief, in short it was apparent to the whole world that this was the guilty man. Then the true thief was discovered, and the innocent neighbor no longer looked remotely guilty.

grandma pays her respects

Grandma was fond of a pretty temple a little way off where we took her by car. It was the custom to rub a little gold leaf on the Buddha images by way of an offering. I noticed that she always stuck her gold on the back of the Buddha and asked Lek why. "She's very modest. We believe that if you stick the gold leaf on Buddha's back only he will know of your good deeds."

on having no head

James suggested I tell you how we met. There was a man who did the round of Buddhist societies with a lecture called, "On Having No Head." Part of the lecture involved a little experiment in which the audience divided into pairs each of whom were given a paper bag with the end cut off. You and your partner were to stare at each other down the tube. I happened to be sitting next to James and found myself gazing at him in the face. When he saw that, like him, I was trying not to laugh, he mouthed, "What a load of *******." The lecturer was not best pleased, but it started a friendship that lasted 30 years and spanned the world. Not bad going for a paper bag.

what pitcher?

Zen master Po-chang had so many students
that he had to open a new monastery. To decide
who should be in charge he called all his monks
together a set a pitcher before them.

"Without calling it a pitcher, tell me what it is."
"You couldn't call it a piece of wood," said the
most senior monk.

Then the cook jumped up, kicked over the
pitcher and walked away. He was put in charge
of the new monastery.

stoned

"Look at that rock," said the master,
"is it inside or outside your mind?"
"According to our beliefs everything is the
objectification of mind," said the pupil confidently.
"Then your head must be very heavy with such a
great rock in it," retorted the master.

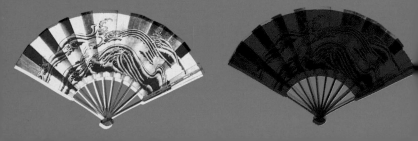

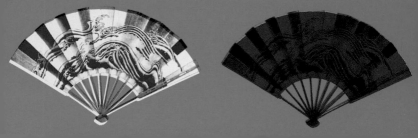

189

in praise of confucius

My Chinese teacher was a Buddhist with a respect and affection for Taoism. One day I let slip that I'd never been able to feel much enthusiasm for Confucius who I'd always thought of as a rather unspiritual figure who was at odds with all I believed. I was amazed that she became angry. The Oriental ability to hold different beliefs that, to a Westerner, would be mutually exclusive is to me a source of genuine wonder and admiration. It's not hard to see why Buddhists have never been inclined to religious persecution.

the workings of karma?

Lek wanted me to tell you how we met. She said if you didn't believe in karma after that, you never would. I ran out of London's Science Museum, where I worked, and blundered into three Thai girls looking for their embassy. I gave them directions and rushed on to catch my train. A week later I bumped into the same trio outside King's College, Cambridge. Not too strange so far, these are two of the biggest tourist attractions in England. A couple of weeks after that I met an old friend I hadn't seen for years who announced he'd married a Thai girl. He invited me to dinner. When I arrived, guess who the other guests were.

191

knowledge

One who knows does not speak,
One who speaks does not know.

TAO TE CHING

192

repellent disgust

The Zen master Bankei admitted a group of lepers as
students. He even shaved their heads with his own hands.
An onlooker, repelled by the sight of the master touching
lepers, brought water for him to wash the pollution from his
hands, but Bankei scolded him.
"Your disgust offends me much more than their condition,"
he retorted.

193

strangers on a train

I was in London having lunch with a lama I knew, when he said, "Do you know that, even before I knew you, you had helped me?"

I was surprised. I'd always been under the impression that he'd done all the helping.

"You remember that before we knew each other we used to travel on the same train from Cambridge? Well, one day I arrived late and couldn't get a seat. That didn't bother me because I was too worried about what I was doing in this country. Teaching Buddhism here seemed like banging my head against a brick wall. Then I happened to glance over your shoulder and saw that you were reading a book on Buddhism. I can't tell you how much that encouraged me."

194

a good day?

It is a Zen saying that every day is a good day. Can you tell yourself that on a miserable Monday morning in January and still smile while you say it?

195
the archer

Chuang-tzu tells a story of an archer. While he was competing for a leather girdle his aim was true, when the prize was a bronze vessel his aim started to stray. When the prize was gold he lost his aim altogether.

the horse buyer

Po Lo used to procure horses for the Duke of Mu.
As he got old the duke asked him to recommend a
successor. He named Chiu-fang Kao. The duke sent
him to look over a horse he'd heard about. When he
returned the duke asked, "What sort of horse is it?"
"Oh, it's a dun-colored mare."

When the horse arrived it was a black stallion.
The duke was furious and summoned Po Lo.
"That friend of yours is useless!" and he told him
what had happened.

"Excellent! Has he really got as far as that? He is
worth a thousand of me for he sees the inner nature
of the horse and ignores insignificant details."

The horse did indeed turn out to be an excellent animal.

LIEH-TZU

197

what is buddha?

"A dried shit stick."
YUN-MEN

agree to disagree

Mary-Beth announced that she was going back to the States. Somewhat to our surprise, we were sorry to see her go. At first we'd seen her as rather silly and interfering but, though she'd never given up in her attempts to reclaim us all for whatever sect it was she belonged to (we were never exactly sure), over the months we'd discovered that you can still be friends with someone even if you profoundly disagree with them. There were smiles and tears all round as she left.

199
wishful thinking

Lek's youngest had been learning about puja,
the act of making an offering to Buddha, at school.
She explained to me about the three joss sticks
(for the Buddha, the Teaching, and the Sangha or
community of monks), and then about the candle
that represents enlightenment. She made her way
through the traditional prayer (I take my refuge in
the Buddha, I take my refuge in the Dharma, I
take my refuge in the Sangha) without a mistake.
Then she looked a bit puzzled.
"What's wrong?" I asked.
"I think when you've finished you're allowed to blow
the candle out and make a wish, but I'm not sure."

200
self-knowledge

It's surprising how easy it is to see another's bad karma and how hard it is to see one's own!

preparation

Little Monkey took to walking around
holding her nose. I asked her why but she
just went shy on me, so I asked her big sister.
"She wants to be a farang [Westerner]
like you in her next life, but she
thinks the nose will need
a lot of work!"

202

the benefits of death

Tzu-kung was weary and said to Confucius,
"I long for a good rest."
"There is no rest in this life," replied the sage.
"Is there no rest anywhere, then?"
"Oh yes, look at the graveyards, you can
find rest there."
"Then death is great indeed," exclaimed Tzu-kung, "for
it gives rest to the good but makes evil people cower."
"Yes," agreed Confucius, "people only think of the evils
of death and don't give a thought to the benefits."

LIEH-TZU

mad dog

Lek's middle daughter was bitten by a rabid dog and we were all worried about her. She needed a series of painful injections, which she took very bravely. In fact she was quite proud of herself and tended to show off about her courage under the needle. One day, I took her to the monastery shrine and she saw some monks we knew quite well. She immediately cornered them and told them all about the dog bite. The monks were a bit nervous as she was getting to the age where she wasn't exactly a little girl any more and the rules about contact with women are strict. Still all went well until she decided to bring her act to its climax.

"Do you know where they have to inject you?"

Unfortunately they didn't.

"In the belly. Right here. Look!"

la dolce vita

Tread softly; live gently.

temper, temper

A man went to a Zen master for advice.

"I have an ungovernable temper," he said, "what can I do?"

"That's interesting. Show me."

"I can't. It just comes on unexpectedly."

"In that case it isn't yours at all."

206

divine comedy

"Even the gods love jokes."

PLATO

staying cheerful

A few of the monks found Sean's natural jollity unsuitable for monastic life. Monks are supposed to be withdrawn, aloof, and free from the temptations of the senses. Sean was happy and outgoing. He liked people and he felt compelled to let them know it. Although the abbot tried to restrain his pupil's exuberance he was always quick to defend Sean. "He has more trouble than the others because everything here is strange to him. But what I like is that he tries and tries and tries. He never gives up and he always stays cheerful. What more can you ask?"

buddha announces his rebirth

And on Lord Buddha, waiting in that sky,
Came for our sakes the five sure signs of birth,
So that the Devas knew the signs, and said
"Buddha will go again to help the World."
"Yea!" spake He, "Now I go to help the world
This last of man times; for birth and death
End hence for me and those who learn my Law..."

"THE LIGHT OF ASIA" EDWIN ARNOLD

enlightenment

Professor D.T. Suzuki was largely responsible for the arrival of Zen in the West. One day someone asked him what enlightenment was like. "Just like ordinary life," he replied, "only two inches off the ground."

210

on not withdrawing

The perfect man can transcend the limits of the human and yet not withdraw from the world. Those who would benefit mankind from deep forests or lofty mountains are simply unequal to the strain upon their higher natures.

CHUANG-TZU

talking and listening

When you have a talking mouth you have no listening ears. When you have listening ears you have no talking mouth.

GETTAN

212

a breath of fresh air

The breath has a special place in Buddhism, as it is central to the practice of meditation. It is said that one day the senses were discussing which of them was most important. They decided to go away one at a time to see how the body managed without them. Sight went, but the body managed. Hearing went, but the body survived. Smell went, but the body didn't suffer. At last Breath asked to join in. The moment it left the body all the others screamed for it to return.

do what thou wilt

"Do what thou wilt shall be the whole of the law,"
is supposed to be the Satanists' motto. Maybe
Buddhists should rip it off. It's not that they believe
in unbridled self-indulgence. What they really
believe in is taking responsibility for your actions.
Do what thou wilt...and pay for it!

ego

The Yellow Emperor asked: "If my spirit returns
through gates it came from, and my body goes
back to the earth from which it sprang, where
does the Ego then exist?"

LIEH-TZU

215

cold-comfort farm

I went with Lek's husband and another friend to stay in a hill-tribe village. It didn't sound like five-star comfort. No running water, no toilets, bamboo and grass huts to live in. We set out from Chiang Mai, the northern capital, and traveled for many miles in a Land Rover over bumpy, rutted mountain tracks. It was hot and dusty. By the time we eventually got there we were tired, hungry, filthy, and sore from sitting on hard seats for hours. Suddenly the simple accommodation our hosts offered seemed like five-star comfort after all.

216

ave maria

One of the old monks died suddenly. Sean came upon him in the garden having apparently just conked out from extreme old age. When I saw Sean he looked upset.

"I suppose it was a bit of a shock for you?" I ventured.

"Yes, but that's not the problem."

"So why do you look so worried."

"Because when I found him I'd crossed myself and got off a couple of Hail Marys before I knew what I was doing!"

217

work

Get off your behind and do something useful! The work is part of the koan.

HAKUIN

218

invitation to balmoral

Through a strange train of events I found myself
invited to a private party on a small island owned
by the king's mother. In Thailand she was as
revered as the Queen Mother was in England.
Before being introduced I was politely checked
out by one of her staff.

"Have you ever been to Scotland?" he asked.

"I grew up there," I told him.

"Have you often stayed at Balmoral?"

"No, not often. In fact, not at all."

"Has your queen not invited you?"

"No, not so far."

"It was probably an oversight. I sure she will
invite you soon."

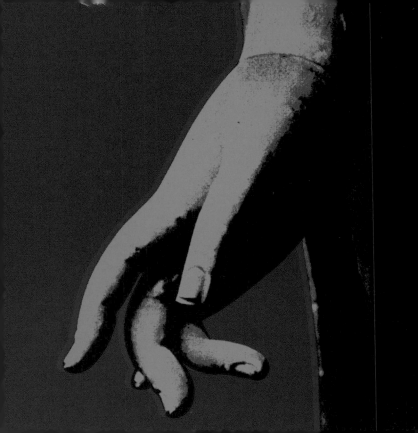

219
gifts

Your smiles are not just for you; they are your gift to the world.

learned smiles

Thailand is sometimes called "The Lands of Smiles."
My friend taught in a school for young ladies. They
learned deportment and one of the exercises involved
sitting gazing into a mirror and learning to smile constantly.
I thought this a rather pointless exercise. What was the use
of a smile that did not come from the heart? "Oh no,"
replied Lek, "it works the other way around. If you smile
enough it will eventually reach your heart."

the lost sheep

When I told my headmaster of my interest in
Buddhism he tried to take it well. He was a
humane man with a deep interest in education,
but he was also a staunch upholder of traditional
values and deeply suspicious of the ideas
flooding in from the East.

"It's excellent for young people to try out new
ideas," he said bravely, "but in the end I expect
you'll return to the fold."

Over thirty years later I'm still AWOL.

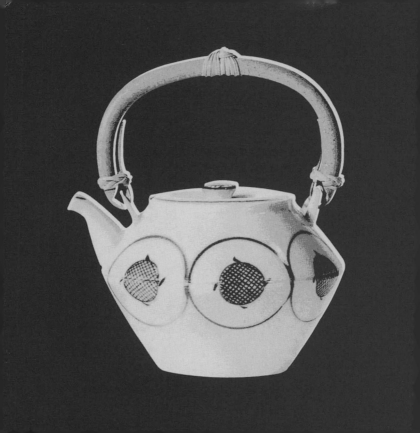

222

limited choice

I was in Jerusalem on business and hailed a taxi.
The driver introduced himself as George and, by
the crucifix around his neck, I gathered he was a
Palestinian Christian.
"Are you a Christian, a Jew, or a Muslim?" he asked.
This happens to me all the time. I look too dark for a
Brit and people get confused.
"I'm a Buddhist," I replied with a smile.
There was a pause.
"Look, guy, I'm not going to shoot you, I just want to
know whether you're a Christian, a Jew, or a Muslim."

223

unexpected meeting

I found Israel utterly confusing. The politics, the violence, the intrigue, the religion, all of it conspired to baffle me. One day I visited the Holocaust memorial of Yad Vashem and, walking through the garden of remembrance, saw an old Japanese Zen monk approaching me. The sudden feeling of recognition was so great that I gave him a beaming smile as he passed. I bet he still wonders why.

224

god is great

Because Jerusalem was hot I'd get up and meditate in the cool of the early morning, just in time for the call to prayer. I liked the sound of it very much and just let it become part of my zazen. I mentioned this to George who by this time had become my personal taxi driver. He was horrified.
"It's not music you know. It's about Muslims praying. If your Buddha finds out what you've been up to I bet you'll be in real trouble."

225
time for tea

One day I was telling Lek the continuing story of
Sean's delicate stomach. No matter how hard he tried
he couldn't shake off the diarrhea that had plagued
him since he arrived. The Old Lady was sitting with
us and immediately called a passing student to go to
the sick bay and fetch something. It turned out to be
tea. Not the green watery stuff the Thais are fond of
but real black tea.
"Tell him to drink this as strong as possible and
without milk or sugar," she ordered.
To our amazement the tea put a smile back on Sean'
face and calmed the erratic workings of his insides.

the wanderer

In Cambridge there was a man who shaved his head, dressed in robes, and carried his few possessions in a bundle on his back He lived in an outbuilding loaned to him by a local vicar. Sometimes he'd ask passersby for small change, though he didn't seem like the usual sort of beggar. I never saw him drunk, nor did he sit around with the down and outs. He looked just like a mendicant out of some Taoist or Zen tale. Who was he? Opinions vary widely and no one agrees on the truth. Was he a holy man? A dropout? A crank? It was hard to tell. If you'd met a Zen master or Taoist would you have recognized him? I used to think I would, but now I'm not so sure.

227
the clothes of the dog

A man went out wearing one set of clothes and got caught in a downpour. He made his way to a friend's house and borrowed a change of clothes. When he returned home his dog didn't recognize him and began to snarl. The man was angry and went to beat the dog. A passing Buddhist monk, feeling compassion for the dog, told the man to stop and explain what was wrong. When he heard the story he said, "You can't blame the dog. After all, what would you do if he went out a black dog and came home white?"

meditating aussies

I went with some friends on a cycling holiday in Suffolk.
We stopped at a Youth Hostel because we couldn't
afford anything more comfortable. In the common room
were two young Aussies who sat meditating. People
always assume that while you meditate you're
somewhere on Planet Janet.
"Where do you think they're from?" asked someone.
"They're Aussies, they've got flags on their backpacks."
"What are they doing?"
"I dunno, looks like meditation or something."
"How long do they do that?"
"How should I know?"
The girl opened one eye.
"Shaddup, willya?" and carried on meditating.

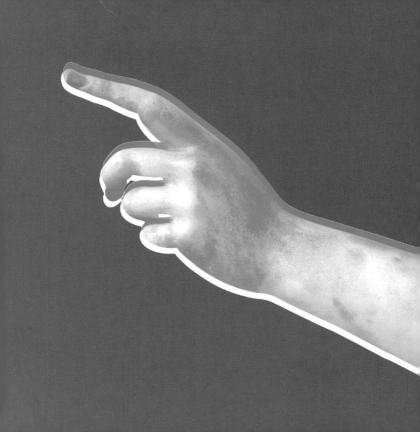

buddha and the ascetics

Before his enlightenment Buddha joined a group of ascetic monks who sought spiritual progress through mortification of the flesh. He sat, starving and unwashed, trying to reach enlightenment through the most severe privations. At last he realized that this was not the way. He got up, went and bathed, put on clean clothes and had a meal. The ascetics were outraged and accused him of backsliding. But Buddha was happy because at last he had seen the way forward.

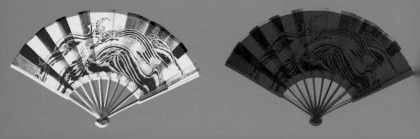

apples not opium

We visited the hill tribes up in the Golden Triangle. Lek told me that the king had started a project to teach them to grow apples instead of opium. It didn't sound like a winner to me. Why grow apples if they can grow drugs?

"Where you come from, drugs are expensive and apples are not. But you can't grow apples in the south because it's too hot. Up here in the mountains it's cool and the apples grow well and are worth a lot of money. Poppies grow like weeds up here and the farmers get almost nothing for opium. You must learn to adjust your values!"

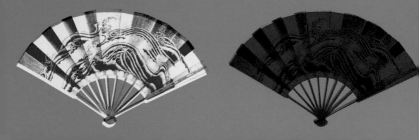

231
the moving finger

There is a Zen story about a master who, whenever anyone asked him about Zen, would just hold up one finger in reply. His young attendant rather liked the look of this and took to doing it whenever the master was not around. One day he got caught and the master seized the boy and cut off his finger. The boy fled screaming but, just then the master called him and, as he turned round, he held up one finger. At that moment the boy was enlightened.

James who, like me, had grown up in Scotland thought about this story for a while.

"You know, that's the difference. If he'd been Scots he'd have held up one finger and wagged it."

232
bargain buddha

I was in the late night market at Chiang Mai
when I saw a Buddha I really liked the look of.
He was on a stall owned by a pretty girl
dressed as a member of the Meo tribe.
The Meo are famed as tough bargainers.
"How much?" I asked her.
She named a fancy price.
"Far too much," Lek's husband muttered.
The girl heard him.
"Don't tell him that, you stinking cholera corpse
rotting in your own shit!" she screamed.
She turned to me with her sweetest smile.
"Now, what will you offer me for this holy image
of our Lord Buddha?"

233

elemental conflict

When water and fire wage war, the water
will be the victor.

ANON

234

giving up

I love the story of the Zen monk who tried for years to find enlightenment without success. Eventually he decided to give up. He thought that if he made himself useful around the monastery he would at least help others in their quest for enlightenment. Immediately he made this decision he became enlightened.

bonny buddhas

Edinburgh might seem an odd place to meet Buddha for the first time. What people forget is that, in the days of empire, the Scots put themselves about a bit. Have you ever wondered why so many West Indians have Scots name? Exactly. So, when I was young and living in the Edinburgh suburb of South Morningside, there were innumerable elderly widows whose homes were decorated with knickknacks brought home by their husbands from the Far East. I always liked the Buddhas especially, but had no idea that the feeling was going to be mutual.

using the sutras

Not long after James went home to England he was
out late one night when he collided with a gang of drunken
louts. They quickly surrounded him and started to jeer
and make threats.

"At first I had no idea what to do," he told me, "if I insulted
them back they'd have beaten me up. If I'd pleaded with
them they would certainly have beaten me up."

"So what did you do?"

"I had an idea. I started to recite one of the sutras."

"What?"

"I know it seems daft. But all that Sanskrit confused the
hell out of them. They didn't know what to make of it."

"What happened?"

"After a while they'd called me all the names they
could think of and they just wandered off."

the bearded foreigner

Bodhidarma came from India and is always depicted as fiercely bearded. One day Wakuan saw a picture of him and demanded, "Why does that fellow have no beard?"

238
the daruma doll

Such is life,
Seven times down,
Eight times up.

(The irrepressible Daruma doll is weighted in the
bottom so it can never be knocked over.)

cremation

Tragically one of the girls at our school died of meningitis. No one enjoys funerals, but the teachers seemed to be in a complete tizzy. You can't talk to Thais about anything unpleasant; it's just not done to discuss such things. With the benefit of complete ignorance I tried to jolly everyone along. I saw the Old Lady giving me one her grimmer smiles and asked her what the matter was. She didn't

share the national obsession with avoiding bad news.

"The girl is to be cremated," she told me.

"Yes, but Buddhists are usually cremated, what's so bad about that?"

"She was from the country; it will be a traditional cremation on an open pyre. Sometimes, as the fire takes hold, the sinews tighten and the body sits up in the flames."

Now I knew why everybody was worried and, frankly, I didn't blame any of them.

240
accountant's karma

Many Thais approaching old age try to perform
meritorious deeds to wipe out their past sins and
help them get a good rebirth. The abbot used to
get really frustrated.

"Why can't they understand" he fumed, "that a
bad deed brings bad consequences and a good
deed brings good ones? Karma isn't a branch of
accountancy, you can't cancel your debts by
making large deposit before you die!"

241

too much

Governing a large state is
like boiling a small fish.

TAO TE CHING

242

the dreaded "gloop"

We went to stay at a wildlife park where tigers were said
to roam free. I saw a spot not far from our camp where I
thought it would be nice to sit and meditate so, after I'd
unpacked, I set off on my own. Thais cannot understand
the idea of solitude. Everyone does absolutely everything
together. One of their favorite English expressions is, "We
going in gloop." Lek's niece saw me set off alone and was
immediately alarmed. Why would I willingly walk off alone?
Decency forbade that a teenage girl should rush after a
man to keep him company. She thought quickly.
I'd just started my meditation when I heard a rustling in
the bushes behind me. Could it be tigers? No, it was the
girl with a posse of about a dozen little kids.
"We have come in gloop," they announced, "to be
your company!"

243

kalpas

In Hinduism and Buddhism a kalpa is a vast measure of time. It is said that you should imagine a huge rock several hundred feet in each direction. Once every hundred years an angel descends and wipes the rock gently with the tip of its wing. The time it takes to wear the whole rock away is a kalpa.

"That," said James, "shows that there must have been Buddhist missionaries to Britain."

"How do you work that out?"

"No one could imagine such a period of time unless they had waited for a British train."

the full lotus

Have you ever tried the full lotus position? Or even the slightly less agonizing half lotus? There are people who believe you can't meditate without sitting with your legs crossed. Ignore them. Sit comfortably. Crossed legs are painful and dangerous (they restrict the circulation and encourage blood clots). Relax. Sit on a chair or, like me, on the end of your bed. Your meditation will improve enormously once it's no longer a form of torture.

245

revolution

There was a small, bloodless military coup. Even so there
were roadblocks everywhere manned by heavily armed
soldiers. Lek hung extra Buddha medallions in the car for
protection. She also went to her brother-in-law, who was an
officer in the Thai Royal Air Force, borrowed one
of his spare peaked caps, and hung it on the rear view
mirror to show that we were loyal to the armed forces.
We got stopped anyway. The soldier looked sinister in
shades and with his machine gun cradled in his arm.
"Where you from?" he asked me brusquely.
"England."
"London?"
"Quite near London."
"My aunty live in Pinner. You know Pinner?"
"Yes, it's very nice."
"Okay, you can go now."

a bigger buddha

Nong was a country cousin who lived with us during term time. One day I saw her at the family shrine making her offerings to the big Buddha in the middle. "Why are you making your puja to him?" I asked, "I thought that little bronze one was your favorite." "Yes, he is, but this time I need a really big favor and the bronze one can't manage on his own."

247

a nice cup of tea

In the old days a Zen master would drive his pupil to the brink of distraction in the quest for enlightenment. One pupil had finally reached the stage where he no longer knew what to do. All the concepts he had relied on all his life had been swept away.

"Now," said the master, "there is nothing left for you but to have a cup of tea."

The pupil was enlightened.

verse and worse

About the time Salman Rushdie gained notoriety with his
Satanic Verses I was running a small publishing company.
A man approached me with a novel and I agreed to read
the manuscript. It was a torrid tale in which a secret society
of Tibetan lamas got up to all sorts of unlikely adventures.
It wasn't badly written but the story was just nonsense.
I asked him why he'd come up with that particular plot.
"Well, you know about Salman Rushdie?"
"Yes, of course."
"I thought if he could be famous for insulting Islam I
might get famous if I was persecuted by Buddhists."
I pointed out that, while he might well hurt and offend
many people, he didn't stand a hope of being pursued
by vengeful lamas.
"Oh well," he grinned ruefully, "it was worth a try."

joshu and the dog

Buddhists believe that all creatures have Buddha
nature. One day a monk asked the Zen master
Joshu if a dog had Buddha nature.
"Mu!" he said. It means "No."
It became one of the great Zen koans.

empty mind

A pupil approached his master.
"Master, I no longer have anything on my mind."
"Then throw it out!"
"If I have nothing on my mind how can I throw it out?"
"Then carry it out."

evangelical fervor

I was walking with Yukiko in Cambridge when
she noticed a couple of students waving at her
from the other side of the street.
"Who are they?"
"Oh, they're Christians, they invited me to one
of their meetings and it was very interesting."
The couple dodged the traffic and approached us.
"Hi," said Yukiko, "I was just telling my friend
about the meeting I went to."
They smiled encouragingly at me.
"Maybe you'd like to come along to the next one?"
Before I got a chance to answer Yukiko broke in:
"Yes, that's a great idea. Then we could invite you
to one of our Buddhist meetings."
To her surprise they made their excuses and left.

252
buddha.com

Modern Buddhism thrives on the Internet and by
e-mail, especially in the West. Buddhists are often few
and far between in Europe or the United States and
often feel rather isolated. Modern communications
have helped to forge a worldwide community. I'd like
to give e-mail and the www a special smile.

253

buddha bashing

When I was a young boy I made the mistake of asking
my primary-school teacher about Buddha. I gathered
that he was definitely not a member of the Church of
Scotland and was very idle (or that, at least, is what I
thought she'd said). Since she often said as much about
me I felt we probably had a lot in common.

buddha's compassion

"…the good Lord Buddha seated him
Under a jambu tree, with ankles crossed—
As holy statues sit—and first began
To meditate this deep disease of life,
What its far source and whence its remedy.
So vast a pity filled him, such wide love
For living things, such passion to heal pain,
That by their stress his princely spirit passed
To ecstasy…"

"THE LIGHT OF ASIA" EDWIN ARNOLD

vipassana

The monks used to teach a form of
meditation in which you sit and watch
your thoughts as they arise and then
see them pass away. It's an odd
experience. If you're worried
or disturbed in some way, sit
quietly and try to grasp the worry
and hold it tight. See what happens.
The thoughts that previously plagued
you will now try to slip away like eels
escaping capture. The harder you try
to stay worried, the more difficult it
becomes. Suddenly the worry that
seemed to weigh on you like a rock is
no more substantial than a bit of mist.

256

long-tail boat

A long-tail boat has a small motorcar engine, a very long prop shaft, and a tiny propeller on the end. To steer it you just swing the whole engine around on a pivot. They can go very fast indeed.

At times of high stress Thais sometimes take the Buddha amulet round their neck and suck it. There is a superstition that if you die with Buddha in your mouth you go straight to nirvana.

We were in the back of the boat and getting nervous. The young lad in charge was throwing us back on forth across the water with far more confidence than skill. I saw Lek take her Buddha and slip it into her mouth.

"Will that help?" I shouted above the roar of the engine.

No answer. I tried again. Still no answer. When we eventually stopped, unharmed, I asked why she wouldn't reply.

"I was trying hard not to chew," she said.

257
shunryu suzuki

Suzuki wrote *Zen Mind, Beginner's Mind,* which is one of the great books on Zen. I've owned many copies over the years and always end up giving them away to friends. More than anyone else he made Zen seem attainable to ordinary people who did not want to enter into the monastic life. I always wished I could have met him but, sadly, he died when I was still young. Even so, I have always felt close to him and welcome the opportunity to give him a smile.

love story

Richard was a friend of ours and another Buddhist convert. During his stay in Bangkok he'd met and married a pretty young prostitute, which made things a bit awkward. To Richard she looked like any other Thai girl but to the various women in our circle she might as well have had "hussy" tattooed on her forehead. Then, to everyone's disbelief, Richard was killed in a car crash. Cynical people had muttered that the girl merely saw her wealthy Westerner as a meal ticket. They were taken aback when she was inconsolable at his death and, rather than take up with another man, continued to live alone as a young widow.

259

optical illusion

Have you ever seen that optical illusion where two black faces change into a white vase? I always think it's a good analogy for Zen. It's not that Zen disputes the way the world is. It's just that we look at it the wrong way. The normal view causes us pain and discontent. Adjust your view and you find peace and satisfaction.

260
my favorite buddha

Many, many years ago I bought a Buddha in an
Oriental curio shop. We've never been apart since.
He's quite small, made of dark wood, and stands
holding a rosary. He smiles, just as all Buddhas do,
but his is a much broader smile than usual and,
because he lost an eye some years ago, he appears
to be winking too. My Thai friends never liked him
much. He doesn't look religious enough. He seems
to be enjoying life and to expect you to join him. They
even tried to tell me that he wasn't a Buddha at all
and, technically, they may be right. But to me, he is
just the right sort of Buddha.

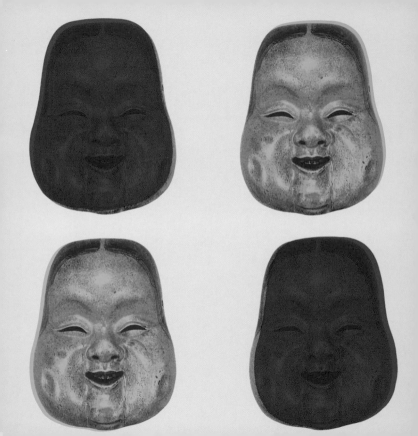

would I like to be a monk?

"Why don't you become a monk?" asked Sean.
"What me?"
"Yes, you'd make a very good monk."
"Sean, I would make the worst monk in the history
of monkhood. I drink alcohol, I eat meat, I enjoy
sex, and I have a problem with authority."
"But that's the point, being a monk would help
you overcome all those things."
"No it wouldn't. I'll deal with all my shortcomings
in my own way, thanks. Anyway, why the sudden
interest in my spiritual welfare?"
"I just thought you'd be good company. And they'd
have someone worse than me to disapprove of."

fortune telling

Buddhist temples often offer services that haven't much to do with Buddhism. My favorite was the fortune-telling sticks. Like horoscopes they were rubbish, but you just couldn't resist having a go. There's a bamboo cylinder full of thin wooden sticks. You take hold of it in both hands and shake it gently back and forth. Now comes the good bit: eventually one of the sticks climbs out of the cylinder and falls on the floor. It bears a number and, on a table nearby, you will find a slip of paper with a fortune that has the same number on it. Simple fun, but it never fails to amuse.

263

instant enlightenment

A young Swiss guy turned up at talks
given by the abbot and listened intently.
Sean would give a running translation
in English for any foreigners who were
interested. Afterward we struck up a
conversation with him and discovered
that he'd come, of course, in search of
enlightenment. He got it all planned out.
He would spend twelve months getting
enlightened and would then go home
and get on with his life.

264
belief

Religion is the fashionable substitute for belief.
OSCAR WILDE

265

work out your own salvation

I was at a conference during which a vicar warned us solemnly against the dangers of what he called "pick 'n' mix religion." Apparently he was worried that people were taking on board ideas that they had found in "exotic" religions such as karma, rebirth, and enlightenment. They were then mixing these into heady spiritual cocktails. This dangerous development, he insisted, was at the expense of "the religions of faith." Now, while it's true that you can find some people with a very colorful set of beliefs, is this really such a bad thing? Instead of being worried that people are having unorthodox ideas, shouldn't we be happy that they are interested enough to think for themselves?

zazen

For some reason many people get really fearful about trying Zen meditation. They imagine that they are playing with the occult or, at the very least, meddling dangerously with the workings of their own mind. You can dismiss the first fear without any compunction at all. But what about the second? Zazen will, in time, make a big difference, and once you get to a certain stage you will continue down that road even if you try to give it up. On the other hand you know from your own experience that zazen is immensely valuable. So what do you say? One of my friends had agonized so long over whether or not to give it a go I finally said, "For goodness sake, all you need to do is sit on your backside and breathe! How hard can it be?"

267
the melting pot

Cambridge is a cosmopolitan sort of place. One day a missionary of some sort called at the front door.

"You won't have much luck in this street," I told him.

"Why not?"

"Next door that side are Irish Catholics and the other side are Hindus."

"I'll try further up the street."

"No good. The next lot are Greek Orthodox and after them there's a Polish Catholic and the people at the end are Chinese Buddhists."

He suddenly eyed me with new interest.

"Buddhists just like me," I added quickly.

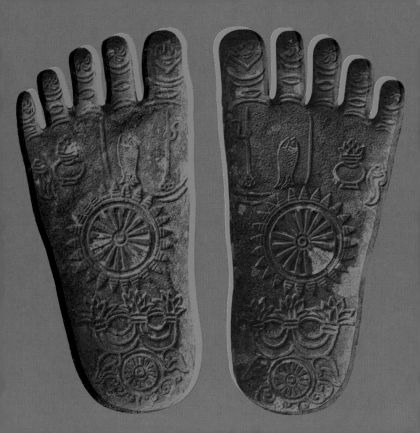

268

driving to win

Like the British, Thais drive on the left. This is where all similarity ends. Thai driving involves flinging your vehicle forward while leaning on the horn and ignoring oncoming traffic until the last possible second. It's no wonder that people get the monks to bless their cars! The crossing near our house was particularly lethal. People rushed at from all sides and at full speed. One day, as the usual carnage was in progress, some monks decided to cross. There was a squeal of brakes and everyone put their hands palm to palm and bowed while the holy men made their sedate progress. Then, the very second they had crossed, Lek gunned the engine, let in the clutch and shot across before anyone had time to blink.

the lost lecture

I was in the late-night market in Chiang Mai when an elderly Chinese couple came up to me smiling broadly. "We're so glad to meet you," they enthused. "We were intrigued by the sound of your paper on the development of Buddhism in the West. We're looking forward to hearing you tomorrow." They shook my hand with great warmth and wandered off. Which left me a tad confused, for I had written no such paper and was not scheduled to speak at any conference.

270
persistence

I got an e-mail from Sean the other day with a cartoon attached. It showed a heron trying to swallow a frog. The frog, however, had hold of the bird by the throat and was attempting to throttle it. The caption said, "Never ever give up!"

271

the untouchable

My uncle was a vicar. Once, when we were visiting, I
was introduced to an Indian lady who was staying with
his family. I was fascinated to learn that she was an
untouchable who had been brought to England to be
trained as a teacher so that she could go back and improve
the lot of her people. One evening we got chatting and,
even though she was a Christian, she told me the story of
Buddha asking an untouchable for a drink of water. The
young man had apologized that, though he would be happy
to offer the water, he dared not because, if the Buddha
accepted it, he would lose caste. Buddha thanked him and
took the drink anyway. So, there was the Buddha again!
Funny how he kept touching my life in the oddest places.

don't know

The two most important words in Buddhism are "don't know." If you've ever studied Western philosophy you'll remember that the Problem of Knowledge ("What do we know? How do we know it? How do we know that we know it?") is a favorite subject. Unfortunately, having reached the inevitable conclusion that we don't know anything, our philosophy tends to shy away from the consequences and go off in search of something more interesting. This is a great shame. Grab hold of "don't know" and hang on tight. It's not easy; we are always tempted to consider our opinions as incontrovertible, but if you succeed in hanging on long enough you'll smile when you find that "don't know" is not mere ignorance but something fundamentally important and very exciting.

waiting for buddha

Someone (I forget who) once said that, if you want to see Buddha, just do nothing. That way you'll still be around when he comes again!

making the revolution

When I went to university most people seemed to be involved with some variety of revolutionary socialism. I wasn't much interested because Buddhism was giving me more than enough to think about. One day, as I made my way to a seminar, I was offered the opportunity to buy yet another socialist tract. I'd only just said, "No thanks" when the enthusiastic seller seized me by the shirt and dragged my face to within an inch of his own.

"Why don't you want to help make the Revolution?" he screamed.

Some questions answer themselves.

feed the fish

The monastery had a huge pond in the grounds, which was home to some monster fish. Sean would often be found feeding them scraps (they seemed to eat just about anything). One day I was giving him a hand and remarked on how tame the fish were. They actually liked you to stroke them! Sean smiled, and then looked a bit concerned.

"The trouble is," he confided, "I can never quite put out of my mind what they'd taste like."

276

baby zazen

A young lady appeared on a Zen
e-mail list needing some help. She
was worried that since having a baby
her life had been so full of sleepless
nights, diaper changes, baby walking,
feeding, and a thousand other tasks
that she no longer had time for zazen.
"Don't worry," said a friend, "all
those things are zazen."

277
chingchoks

The chingchok is a very pretty little pale green lizard.
In Thailand they live openly in houses and are always
to be seen scampering up the walls and across the
ceilings. Every room has half a dozen or so. No one
would dream of getting rid of them for the chingchoks
solve problems and have a special place in everyone's
affections. This is because they live on bugs and,
especially, mosquitoes. Slaughtering these pests is, for
many people, unthinkable. On the other hand the
mosquitoes, no matter how hard you try to keep them
out, get indoors and eat you alive. At night the
chingchoks gather near the light fittings and dine at
leisure, leaving everyone else with a clear conscience
and a clear skin.

the volunteer

There was a rumor that Sean had been an IRA
volunteer who had turned to Buddhism as a result of
the things he had experienced in Belfast. Someone
said he was known as "The Butcher of Belfast." I
found it hard to, imagine. True he called me a "Proddy
(Protestant) dog" sometimes, but blithely I assumed
he was joking. So I asked him. He looked grave.
"If I tell you will you promise to keep it to yourself?"
"Yes, of course."
"Okay, then. But if you let on I'll kill you, precepts or
no precepts."
"Fair enough."
"I was training to be a butcher in Belfast."

279

eshun's exit

I've always smiled at the story of the Zen nun, Eshun,
who, realizing that it was her time to die, got some monks
to build a pyre and then climbed up and had it set alight.
As the flames burned higher one of the monks called out,
"Is it hot in there?" to which Eshun replied, "Only an idiot
like you would ask such a question!"

280
a writer's life

Being a writer I have the freedom to go to the gym and work out in the lunch hour when most people are stuck in town. The gym is just beyond the end of my backyard, which is handy. One day, as I was handing over my money, the manager looked awkward and said:

"I hope you not offended but, as you don't work, you're entitled to a concession."

"But I do work. I'm a freelance writer."

"Oh, I see. What are you writing now?"

"A book about Buddhism."

"That's okay, you still get the concession if you only work part-time."

281
baha'i

If anyone deserves a smile it's the followers of the
Baha'i faith who have a fundamental belief in the
value of all religions and the spiritual unity of mankind.
This, you might believe, would be a popular view,
but actually the Baha'is have been ruthlessly
persecuted, imprisoned, tortured, and murdered.
This tells you a lot about the difference between
"religion" and spirituality.

282

this hurts me more than it hurts you

A Zen master was about to thrash his young disciple.
"Does it bother you to treat me like this?" asked the boy.
"Of course, it hurts me more than it hurts you," replied his
master primly. "Lord Buddha tells us to accept nothing that
is not given willingly, so I'm afraid I must decline your
beating," said the boy as he made his escape.

As I may have mentioned, I'm no great
fan of Confucius. Everything about him
seems opposed to my Buddhist/Taoist
outlook. Lek, however, was very keen on
the I Ching, which is very Confucian in
tone. One day the whole family was on
a journey to a distant province when
the train broke down. We were stuck for
ages. Eventually, to pass the time, Lek
decided to consult the I Ching. She does
it the proper way using a bundle of sticks
rather than the lazy three-coin method.
After a long time she came up with the
answer: "Make no move in any direction."

284

the church and the temple

When I came back to England I suddenly found churches were strange places compared to the temples of Thailand. Everybody, including the tourists, seems to enjoy the quiet of a church, often set in pretty scenery and providing a little oasis of calm amid the rush and bustle of daily life. But the contrast with the temples in Bangkok made me smile. Temples are as busy as shops. People come and go all day, every day. They don't smell of musty old hymnbooks and rising damp but reek of incense. They don't have bells only when the volunteer ringers turn up, but allow the wind to ring them or even provide sticks so that visitors can beat them themselves. I miss the temples very much.

cobra in the kitchen

We were woken by screams of our servant girl, who had discovered a cobra on the kitchen floor. Within seconds the entire family assembled to have a look from the safety of the doorway. I rather like snakes, but that doesn't extend to risking a bite from a three-foot cobra. What to do? Killing it was out. Eating meat was one thing, but nothing could be killed intentionally. The plan, therefore, was to encourage it into a pillowcase. The snake was not keen. We abandoned the effort and retired to consider Plan B. Lek went to the family shrine and Ud, our servant, rushed outside to placate the spirits dwelling in our spirit house. Eventually we returned to the kitchen only to discover the cobra curled up happily in the bag. There was a lively discussion about whether Buddha or the house spirits deserved the credit.

buddha's footprint

I was offered the chance to go and see one of Buddha's footprints. I was intrigued. How could they tell after 2,500 years that the print was genuine? When we got there I was even more bemused. The print was about three feet long, shaped like a U, and had toes all the same length. It was, I was assured, without doubt the real thing.

287
all mixed up

The cultural melting pot is something I'm very keen on. It has helped the spread of so many interesting and useful ideas. This is a story I heard from Pete Seeger, the American folk singer.

A man arrived in a new town and wanted a pizza. He asked a passerby who told him that the best pizza in town came from the Chinese restaurant in the main square. He ate the pizza and it was, indeed, excellent. "How come a Chinese restaurant does pizza?" he asked.

"Oh, that's easy," explained the owner, "we have a large Jewish clientele."

meditation for missionaries

We had a letter from Mary-Beth. Having left Thailand and returned home she now decided she'd like to try some form of meditation. She still belonged to her little-known sect but we were wrong about her being the only member because apparently some of her friends had warned her against meditation on the grounds that it would trick her into chanting the names of pagan gods. Lek wrote back. If she wanted to use a mantra, why not use, "Om mani padme hum?" It means, "Behold the jewel in the lotus." If in doubt she could look the meaning up on the Internet or in the library. Mary-Beth thought that sounded okay. As far as I know she's still using it.

289

the doctrine

Those who study the doctrine of the Buddhas will do well to believe and observe all that is taught by them. It is like unto honey; it is sweet within, it is sweet without, it is sweet throughout; so is the Buddha's teaching.

BUDDHA

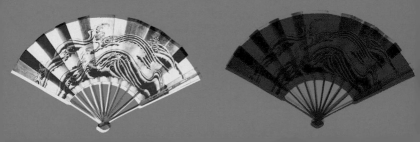

290
chai yen

Thais value chai yen very highly. It means "cool heart," but not in the sense of cold and unfeeling. It refers to the ability to stay calm under stress, not to give in to anger or other violent, destructive emotions. It is a very Buddhist virtue. It is, however, extremely difficult when, just as you're getting a bit worked up, someone whispers, "chai yen" at you. Somehow there is nothing more guaranteed to make your temper much, much worse.

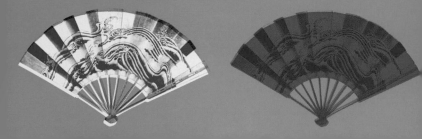

291
dying to know

"Where do we go when we die?" a student asked.
"Why do you think you go anywhere?" answered the
master, "do you think you came from anywhere?"

three in the morning

A man who kept monkeys fed them on bananas. He gave them three in the morning and four in the afternoon. The monkeys were clearly dissatisfied, so he gave them four in the morning and three in the afternoon and then they were happy.

the hinduization of england

Many years ago I met a tiny, elderly Indian gentleman
who had become something of a celebrity by warning
darkly that England was becoming "Hinduized". He was
one of the old school Indians who had been profoundly
impressed by what he considered to be the virtues of the
British Raj and could see nothing but disaster now that
cultural influences were running in the other direction.
At the time I was sure that he was getting things out of
proportion. The number of people interested in Eastern
culture was still comparatively tiny. Nowadays I'm not so
sure. You come across Buddhist and Hindu influences in
the oddest places. He would have been deeply shocked
and saddened at this "decline" in British values. I have to
smile a little. He was a nice old man with our best interests
at heart. What a shame that he saw disaster in one such
a beneficial twist of history.

a protestant buddhist

A friend of the family, a Northern Irish Catholic, was giving me some gentle stick about my Scots-Irish ancestry. It was my ancestors, apparently, who were responsible for the repression of Catholics in the north. I pointed out that, first, I had never been to Ireland and, second, I was a Buddhist. She gave me a pitying smile. "You're still a Protestant at heart and, what's more, you have a Protestant face."

295

evil to him who evil thinks

Lek's brother still didn't care for me much
and he took to dropping little hints that
our relationship was more than merely
platonic. It was silly because, even if
we'd wanted to, it would be hard to find
time to ourselves. There were always
kids, friends, or relatives around. Noy,
however, knew that he was irritating us
so he continued with little snide remarks.
One evening, at dinner, he was at it again
when Lek's husband, a very nice but silent,
bookish sort of man, looked up. "Noy,
you are telling us about you, not them.
Why make yourself into a figure of fun?"

finding your way

Buddhism often seems to be like that tracking game we played as kids. One group would be the quarry and the others would hunt them. To make it more interesting the ones being hunted would leave cryptic signs chalked on walls or trees to show which way they'd gone. You often have to puzzle for a while to work out what they meant. Zen masters are famous for their apparently nonsensical pronouncements. And then, one day, you suddenly think, "Ah, so that's what he meant!"

297

worth living for?

Men will wrangle for religion, write for it, fight for it, die for it, anything but—live for it.

CHARLES CALEB COLTON

buddha's enlightenment

Then he rose—radiant, rejoicing, strong—
Beneath the Tree, and lifting high his voice
Spake this, in hearing of all Times and Worlds:

"Many a house of life
hath held me—seeking ever him who wrought
these prisons of the senses, sorrow-fraught;
Sore was my ceaseless strife!
But now,
Thou builder of this tabernacle—thou!
I know thee! Never shalt thou build again
These walls of pain,
Nor raise the rooftree of deceits, nor lay
Fresh rafters on the clay;

Broka yen thy house is, and the ridgepole split!
Delusion fashioned it!
Safe pass I thence—deliverance to obtain."

"THE LIGHT OF ASIA" EDWIN ARNOLD

a zen painting

Long before there was a vogue for bamboo scroll paintings in the West, I bought one and was captivated by it. A magnolia grew on the very edge of a precipice. Its roots pierced the sparse earth and came out the other side of the overhang. You could not imagine a position more precarious. Although at that time I knew almost nothing about Zen, I recognized this as a Zen painting. Suddenly I understood things that had eluded me for years.

300

the devotee

I'd taken Yukiko and Midoli to visit a
Buddhist temple not far from London.
We were just discussing the shrine
when a young woman, obviously a
Thai, came in. She looked us over
and, deciding that we were foreigners
in need of instruction, informed us:
"This is the Lord Buddha.
He is my God!"
We thanked her
profusely and left.

301
conversation

Zui-Gan called out to himself every day, "Master."
Then he answered himself, "Yes, sir."
"Become sober!"
"Yes, sir."
"And after that, do not be deceived by others."
"Certainly sir!"

MU-MON-KWAN

302
morpheus v. meditation

"You shouldn't be tired," my wife says
accusingly, "you did your meditation."
How do you explain that meditation is
not the same as a quiet nap?

303
busy doing nothing

I arrived for a publishing meeting only to discover
that the lady I had come to see was stuck in traffic.
Her secretary was full of apologies and tried her best
to fill up my time until her boss arrived. Would I like
a coffee? Newspaper? Did I want to make some
phone calls? People have a horror of doing nothing.
Life should be busy, busy, busy. I like quiet times.
I never take anything to read on the train. Life is IT.
It is what our existence is all about. It is something to
be savored with a smile, not rushed through until you
get to the next important bit.

304
miracle monk

Two Zen monks met up on a journey and continued on their way together. Eventually they came to a swollen river and one of them, without pausing, threw his hat on the waters and stood on it to float across. The other, seeing this miracle, said in disgust, "If I'd known that he was that sort of person I'd never have traveled with him at all!"

306

eating together

They say the family that prays together stays together.
I'm not sure about that but I'm a big fan of family meals.
It's a custom that is dying in the West. If you're a Westerner
and your family eats together you're probably Jewish.
There may be nothing apparently "religious" about a family
eating but it's an important part of the glue that sticks
people together. Buddhists, being Oriental (even if only by
adoption), understand the importance of communal meals.
What better occasion to swap a few smiles?

304
miracle monk

Two Zen monks met up on a journey and continued on their way together. Eventually they came to a swollen river and one of them, without pausing, threw his hat on the waters and stood on it to float across. The other, seeing this miracle, said in disgust, "If I'd known that he was that sort of person I'd never have traveled with him at all!"

there's always a way

One day we were about to go to a meeting when one of the household chingchoks fell dead at our feet. In Thailand this is a very bad omen. Theoretically you should cancel your journey immediately. But the appointment was important. What to do? Lek told the servant to take the tiny lizard corpse and dispose of it in the front garden. We tiptoed out the back and made our escape! Superstition? Of course, and nothing directly to do with Buddhism. But there is often something so human-hearted and unfanatical about Eastern people that appeals to me very much. It is a marked contrast to the West where rules are often allowed to get in the way of common sense.

306

eating together

They say the family that prays together stays together.
I'm not sure about that but I'm a big fan of family meals.
It's a custom that is dying in the West. If you're a Westerner
and your family eats together you're probably Jewish.
There may be nothing apparently "religious" about a family
eating but it's an important part of the glue that sticks
people together. Buddhists, being Oriental (even if only by
adoption), understand the importance of communal meals.
What better occasion to swap a few smiles?

307
buddhist chants

An acquaintance of mine bought a CD of Buddhist chants and kept playing it in the background while he worked. He told me proudly that it had brought him peace of mind and increased his creativity. I asked him whether he was interested in Buddhism. No, he said, not especially, but those chants really worked.

308

mendicants

Buddhist literature is full of homeless wanderers who search for the enlightenment outside the formal structure of the monastery. While recognizing that I'm not ready to become one of their number, I have always had a special affection for them. Their spirit of freedom is one of the things that attracted me to Buddhism in the first place. Sometimes, like all of us, they take wrong turnings, but they never cease to search. They get a smile because their search is not just for themselves but also for mortgage-paying, child-raising, homeowners like me.

309

pants trouble

Thai pants are so big that you wind them tightly round your waist and tuck them in firmly. If you have the knack, they won't come undone. I don't have that knack. I was playing soccer with some local lads when my pants ended up around my ankles. Just then a file of monks passed by, eyes firmly on the ground, all but the last one, a young, pale man with freckles and a suspicion of ginger fuzz on his shaven chin. He appeared to be trying, without much success, not to laugh. I swore I'd get Sean later.

310

the view from the watchtower

I used to commute to London by train. There was a man of about my age who always took the opposite seat and, eventually, we got into conversation. (If you're British these things take time.) He seemed to enjoy discussing "The Meaning of Life" and that suited me very well. One day, he said, "Shall I come clean?" and, without waiting for my reply, produced a copy of *The Watchtower*, the Jehovah's Witnesses' magazine. I delved in my briefcase and came up with a book about Buddhism. He looked a trifle disconcerted.

"What's the matter, haven't you met a Buddhist before?"

"It's not just that," he grinned ruefully, "I'm not at all sure what you believe, so I don't know quite how I'm going to convince you that it isn't true."

the old lady at prayer

The Old Lady was tiny, ferocious, and, despite being about 80, had a back as straight as any Buddha. She carried a walking stick because, unlike in the West, being old is considered in Thailand a very honorable state and the stick was her badge of office. She never leaned on it. Occasionally she used it to poke naughty girls in the ankles, an odd form of punishment involving far more shame than actual pain. She went to the temple alone, and always in the early evening when the place was empty. We'd see her car draw up in the lane near our house and her driver open the door.

"I wonder," Lek mused one day, "when she gets in there, who do you think bows to who?"

312

heaven

He who looks only at heaven may
easily break his nose on earth.

CZECH PROVERB

313

frog

An ancient pond
Frog jumps in
Plop!

BASHO'S MOST FAMOUS HAIKU
(FREELY TRANSLATED)

314

are you a buddhist?

I never know whether this question should make me laugh or cry. Buddhism isn't big on labels. You don't have to sign up, take the pledge, get baptized, or wear a special hat. You're even free to disagree with anything you want. The onus is on you to find your own way. Buddha said, "Work out your own salvation with diligence." I used to feel like a Buddhist. Now I feel like a human being engaged in my own spiritual journey. It just so happens that the path I'm on is shared with a heck of a lot of Buddhists.

315

no nonsense

A monk asked Master Tosu, "What is the Buddha?"
"The Buddha."
"What is the Tao?"
"The Tao."
"What is Zen?"
"Zen."

the shock of the new

Before the late 1950s Buddhism in the West had been a sedate affair, confined mainly to elderly and rather serious folk. Then, to their surprise and horror, a whole generation of youngsters descended upon them. Many of them had been inspired by Jack Kerouac whose Dharma Bums had brought Buddhism, and especially Zen, to the attention of the under 25s. The new arrivals were not received with much enthusiasm. Beat Zen was perceived, not entirely unjustly, as having more to do with drugs, sex, and loose living than with Buddhism. But there was much more to it than that. The new generation of Buddhists made mistakes but their desire to make a spiritual journey was genuine enough. Eventually, as some of the more outlandish behavior dropped by the wayside; there was a whole new generation of youngsters eager to learn. Karma works in strange ways.

zen and amida

Pure Land Buddhism is not so well known in the West. Historically it has been most popular among the poorer classes in Japan. The devotees of Amida Buddha have only to call unceasingly upon his name in order to be born into the Western Paradise, a place from which it is easier to find enlightenment. Ironically, the number of people finding enlightenment by this method far exceeds those who find it through Zen. Perhaps the simple, unaffected faith of the Pure Land devotees has something to teach us.

318
the doors

If the doors of perception were cleansed,
everything would appear to man as it is, infinite.

WILLIAM BLAKE

319

boat people

When the Boat People started to arrive from Vietnam I got involved in helping them to settle in the UK. The stories they told of epic journeys in leaky boats, of hunger and thirst, of rape, robbery, and murder by pirates, were truly harrowing. One of the helpers, noticing that the old lady he was talking to wore a crucifix, asked whether her faith had helped her on the journey.

"We prayed to Jesus," she said, "and then we prayed to Buddha. In the end we prayed to anyone who was listening. I suppose someone must have heard because we got rescued."

320

voyage

A ship in the harbor is safe, but
that is not what ships are built for.

ANON

321
previously owned

The Japanese have a distaste for secondhand goods which, they feel, are tainted. Yukiko, who just loved doing everything her mom had told her not to, haunted the secondhand stalls on Cambridge market. One day she outdid herself and bought a Victorian mourning brooch made of jet with a lock of some dead person's hair contained behind glass. I viewed the morbid little curio with distaste but her friend Midoli was convulsed with horror and threatened to leave the house unless she got rid of it. Yukiko grinned happily. "A couple of fine Buddhists you are," she mocked, "frightened by a little piece of death."

bred in the bone

I got an urgent message from Sean. Urgency is not
an Irish notion and certainly not a Thai one. It turned
out that he'd just heard that his mother had died
suddenly. There had only two children in the family
and his sister had married an American and now lived
in Chicago. What should he do? On the one hand, a
monk is supposed to renounce everything, but on the
other the Thais regard family as almost a religion in itself.
Poor Sean was getting some very mixed messages
from his brother monks. After a couple of days of
hesitation he decided to go home for good. He knew
his father wouldn't cope on his own.
"What decided you?"
"Would you believe I traveled all this way to be a
Buddhist and in the end it was good old Catholic
guilt that did for me?"

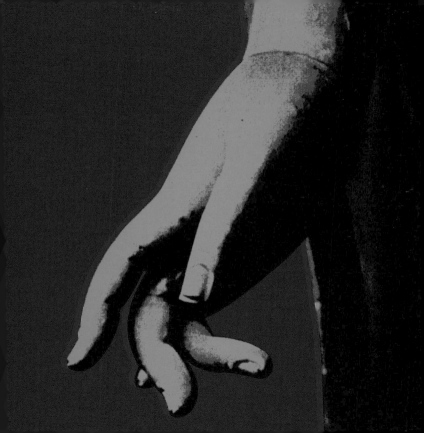

323
man

What is man? An angel, an animal, a void, a world, a nothing surrounded by God, indigent of God, capable of God, filled with God, if it so desires.

BÉRULLE

324
hot dog

Zen Buddhist to hot dog vendor:
"Make me one with everything."
The vendor makes the hot dog, and gives it to
the Buddhist. The Buddhist pays with a twenty.
The vendor turns away, starts to leave.
Zen Buddhist: "Where's my change?"
Hot dog guy: "Change must come from within."

325

least resistance

As the snow gathers on the bamboo leaf, the leaf does not resist. Yet when the snow gets too heavy the leaf, while staying relaxed, gives way and throws off the weight. Non-action in action.

ANON

326

good idea?

The world is our idea.

ANON

embracing the moon

Li Po (say Lee Bor) is one of China's most famous poets and translations of his work have become very popular in the West. My Chinese teacher was so keen on him that she made me learn several of his poems by heart. He was a romantic, a wanderer, and known for being excessively fond of wine. It is said that he eventually drowned when he drunkenly tried to embrace the reflection of the moon in the river. Not a good Buddhist example? No, maybe not, and it is the Taoists who lay claim to him. But all Chinese, and many foreigners, have been attracted by his poetry, his disregard for material things, and the freedom with which he lived his life. He was a special sort of mendicant.

328

a zen garden

Everyone with even the slightest interest in Zen has seen pictures of those strange gardens in which gravel is raked into precise patterns around rocks. They seem to have a fascination even for people who know nothing else about Buddhism. Knowing that I was involved in Zen a colleague showed me the latest craze, a tiny Zen garden in a box, complete with sand, mini rocks, and scaled-down rake. She'd take it out in the lunch break and sit contentedly raking the sand and arranging the rocks. It didn't seem much like Zen to me, but as she seemed to be having such a good time I decided it was best to keep my big mouth shut.

the unreal

Around us are pseudo-events, to which we adjust with a false consciousness adapted to see these events as true and real, and even as beautiful.

R.D. LAING

330

a helping foot

I'd arranged to take Yukiko to a huge exhibition about the history and culture of Japan. We decided to meet near my office in Parliament Square. Eventually she came dashing across the road yelling, "Sorry I'm so late!" It turned out that she'd got lost in Leicester Square and had had to get help.

"I found such a nice old man in Leicester Square," she told me, "and he brought me all the way here."

I was surprised; Londoners are not usually that obliging.

"That's him over there," she pointed.

I turned just in time to catch sight of Michael Foot, then Leader of the Opposition, disappearing into the House of Commons.

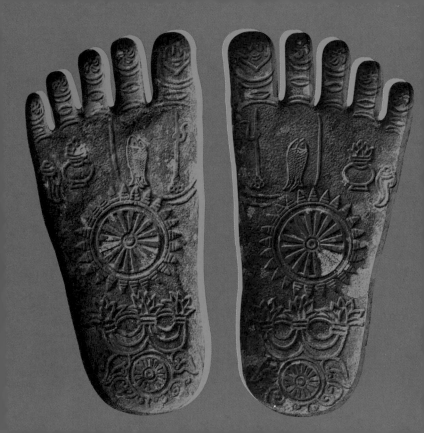

332
camelot

After an introductory talk about the basics of
Buddhism a group had just finished their first
meditation session. I asked them to give me
their impressions.
"I got King Arthur," said Ray proudly.
"Erm, I beg your pardon?"
"King Arthur came to me during the
meditation. He's my spirit guide."
Uh oh. More work needed here, I fear!

growing up

My wife has more integrity than a dog has fleas. In more than twenty years I've never known her do anything mean or underhand. But she hasn't got a religious bone in her body. She just doesn't ever think about that sort of thing. I asked her one day why my involvement in Buddhism hadn't put her off me. "Oh, I always thought you'd grow out of it," she admitted.

commuting

When I returned to England I took a job in London and traveled down each day by train from Cambridge. In those days the journey, which now takes fifty minutes, took a good hour and a half. I met Simon on the train. He was a lecturer in Oriental Studies and we soon found we had a lot in common. Each morning we'd have an interesting chat about Chinese, or Buddhism, or Thai, or Zen. Simon would correct my faulty Chinese by writing with his finger in the condensation on the window. These conversations had an interesting side effect. We were very soon regarded by our fellow travelers as "odd." We never discussed cars, or soccer, or vacations in the Dordogne. And eventually we found that, even when the train was quite crowded, we got seats to ourselves.

the border police

Thailand has some dangerous neighbors and so the borders are constantly patrolled by the Border Police. It's a lonely and dangerous job so people from Bangkok sometimes visit them, bringing a few home comforts and, of course, the ubiquitous Buddha medallions to keep friends and relatives safe. I went along because I was keen to get a ride in a helicopter. It was like living an episode of M*A*S*H. As we got out of the chopper I noticed that the back of my seat had a ragged hole in it.

"What did that?" I asked the pilot.

"The bullet that killed my last passenger," he answered.

I waited for everyone to tell me it was a joke. No one did.

the inexperienced swordsman

A young man approached a master of the sword to
ask for instruction. The master glanced at him and said,
"There is nothing I can teach you for I see that you
are already a master."

The young man protested that, far from being a master,
he had never handled a sword in his life.

"Then there is something very strange, for you look like
a man to whom the sword is second nature."

"Maybe it is this," suggested the young man. "From my
earliest years I have been obsessed by death. I have
thought about it so long and hard that now I have not
the slightest fear of it."

"Ah, yes. Now I can see that you have what is needed
to be a great swordsman."

crossword confessions

You must be careful what you say. My father was a card-carrying atheist and did his best to bring me up disbelieving "all that religion nonsense." One day I asked him if there were any religions that didn't depend on an entirely irrational belief in God. He looked up briefly from his newspaper crossword, muttered "Buddhism" and then went back to 24 Across. You should be especially careful what you say to a child who reads. I went straight to the library and started my journey. Many years later I told him what he'd begun. He rolled his eyes briefly and went back to solving 19 Down.

I never understand the comfort some scientific folk get from reducing life to the word "just." We are "just" animals. We are "just" collections of genes. Our minds are "just" electrical impulses in a blob of jelly. Our world is "just" a speck of dust in a vast universe. It's funny, rather like coming across someone looking down the wrong end of a telescope. Nothing wrong with the instrument, it's just the person who's using it.

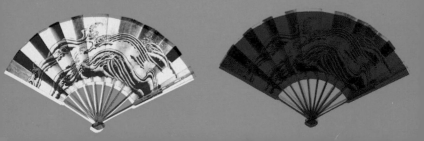

349

finding love

**The astrolabe of the
mysteries of God is love.**
JALAL-UDDIN RUMI

348
that certain feeling

I've never been able to draw. Both my kids are excellent artists but they didn't get it from me. I have no feel for it at all. Stick me in a kitchen, though, and I'm a changed man. I throw ingredients around with confidence, never measure anything, and know just what herbs and spices will produce the effect I'm after. Buddhism requires that sort of feeling too. You don't "get it" if you just read the scriptures and try to follow all the teachings. You have to feel it. If you can feel Buddhism the way you can smell the scents in fresh air, then you start to know what it's all about.

347

the robes

I acquired a new Editorial Assistant called Sophie and, during that sort of "getting to know you" chat that new colleagues go through, the subject of Buddhism came up. She went home and told her family that she worked for a Buddhist. "Does he wear robes?" they chortled. In the following months both her mother and her brother managed to drop by the office and check me out. They were very polite but I could tell that they were both relieved and strangely disappointed that I didn't do anything eccentric.

346

taking it too seriously

I met some Hare Krishnas at Chicago's O'Hare
Airport and, since I had a long wait for my flight,
I got into conversation with them.
It was odd after years of mixing with Buddhists to
hear familiar concepts such as karma and rebirth
being put forward with a sort of puritan zeal. All the
good thoughts were there, but the smile was missing.

345

stone soup

I learned a story like this at primary school and was
surprised to find that another version existed on the
far side of the world.

A wandering monk came to a village and begged for food.
The villagers apologized that their harvest had failed and
they hadn't even enough for themselves. The monk asked
them for a large iron pot, which someone immediately
produced. He had it filled with water and set upon a fire.
Then he threw in a rock and told the villagers that, when it
was cooked, there would be soup enough for everyone.
They were sceptical. Then he asked if anyone had some
salt to flavor it. After that he suggested someone might find
a few leftover vegetables. Then, perhaps, someone might
go to the granary and sweep up the last grains of rice.
When everyone had contributed the bits and pieces they
possessed there was, indeed, enough soup for everyone.

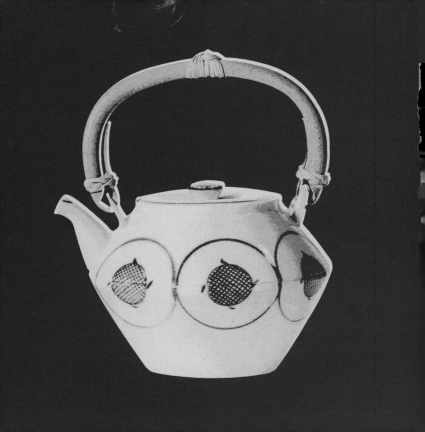

344

the ultimate

"What is the ultimate teaching of Buddhism?"
"You won't understand it until you have it."
SHIH-T'OU

343

how do they know you're a buddhist?

A Catholic friend was quite shocked to find that Buddhists have no special ceremony in which they join the religion, nor do they have to swear to uphold particular doctrines. He couldn't see how anyone could run a decent religion on such a slipshod basis. I tried to convince him that this was a strength, not a weakness. Buddhists are there because they want to be. They are all doing what Buddha instructed when he said, "Work out your own salvation with diligence." People sometimes argue over particular practices or beliefs, but that difference of opinion is always constructive. No one ever sends for the Inquisition.

message in a bottle

Being a writer is a weird occupation. You sit in solitude marshalling your thoughts and then launch them rather like a message in a bottle. You normally have no idea where they go or what effect they have. British readers rarely write back. Whether they enjoy your work or hate it, they say nothing. Americans, or even Australians, are more forthcoming and are quick to complain if they didn't like what they read. But the real satisfaction is when, right out of the blue, you get a letter from somewhere in, say, the middle of Iowa, from someone who felt you spoke directly to their experience. It is strange and wonderful to see that Buddhism is a thriving world community and that, even without being aware of it, you did something that helped it along.

god knows

"Sir, we ought to teach the people that they are doing wrong in worshipping the images and pictures in the temple."
"That the way with you Calcutta people: you want to teach and preach.... Do you think God does not know when he is being worshipped in the images and pictures? If a worshipper should make a mistake, do you think God will know of his intent?"

THE GOSPEL OF SRI RAMAKRISHNA

340

good people

Good people shine from afar,
like the peaks of the Himalayas.

DHAMAPADA

queen maya's dream

Queen Maya had a dream that she
would give birth to the Buddha.
And when the morning dawned, and this
was told, the grey dream-readers said,
"The dream is good!
The Crab is in conjunction with the Sun;
The Queen shall bear a boy, a holy child
Of wondrous wisdom, profiting all flesh,
Who shall deliver men from ignorance,
Or rule the world, if he will deign to rule."

"THE LIGHT OF ASIA," EDWIN ARNOLD

338

kings

The best of all rulers is a shadowy presence to his people. Next comes the one they love and praise. Next comes the one they fear. Next comes the one they dare to ignore.

TAO TE CHING

351
the secret of the flowers

When I first heard the story of Buddha's Flower
Sermon (see page 6), I spent quite a lot of time
wondering what the secret was. It took quite a long
time before it dawned on me that the secret is that
there is no secret.

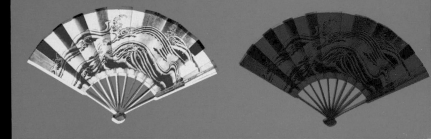

doubting thomas

In every new meditation group there is the Smart Alec. I'm convinced it's the same man who comes each time in a different disguise. When people start discuss their feelings about meditation he'll say, "Oh, so it's really just self-hypnosis, isn't it?" One day I swear my patience will crack and I'll brain him with something.

353
proof

When a mother cries to her sucking babe, "Come here son, I'm your mommy," does the child answer, "Prove to me that I'll shall enjoy your milk!"?

JALAL-UDDIN RUMI

never say "don't"

To someone who was born a Christian the oddest thing about Buddhist monks is their habit of not moralizing. You will be told what sort of behavior helps your progress and what things cause problems but, in all these years, I've never heard the word "don't." It's not that Buddhist scriptures are not full of stern advice; they contain enough to satisfy even the most puritanical heart. But for me one of the best things about Buddhism is its unquenchable faith in its followers and their eventual enlightenment.

355

cooking

If you want to smile, try cooking. There is no trouble that cannot be alleviated by half an hour spent in the kitchen. No wonder the most important job in a Buddhist monastery is that of cook.

if you meet the buddha...

The Japan exhibition was magnificent. It was so huge that they had to show it in two halves, one before Christmas and the other in the New Year. We were viewing one of the exhibits when a rather smart looking lady beside us turned to Yukiko and asked, "Is that a Buddha?"

"You're a Buddha," she replied with her most winning smile, "I'm a Buddha and my friend is a Buddha. But that is a painted piece of wood."

The lady smiled back, but a little uncertainly.

357

change

Change is inevitable. Growth is optional.

ANON

leaving for home

Sean couldn't afford to hop on the first flight out and had to wait around for a cheaper and less direct one.

Despite the sadness of the occasion his last days with us were strangely joyful. Dressed in jeans and a T-shirt, but with his head and eyebrows still shaven, he looked a bit like a chemo patient. He didn't care.

Lek offered him a spare room with us, which he accepted happily. Released from his monk's vows he could now play with the kids. I knew he'd always wanted to, he was the sort of man who'd eventually make a good dad to someone. Before he left he paid one last visit to the abbot. I don't know what was said, but he came back looking happier. Then we took him to the airport and saw him aboard his plane.

359

lack of moral fiber

I was describing to a friend the project I was
involved in to help the Vietnamese Boat People.
A journalist who happened to be working
temporarily in our office overheard.
"I really admire you people," he said. "I mean I
couldn't do what you do. Those Boat People would
drive me nuts. In the army we used to call it "lack of
moral fiber." I mean, they never get up off their butts
and help themselves, do they? Personally I think it's
their religion that makes them like it."
I couldn't quite think of a reply that wouldn't have
violated several important precepts. The idea that
people who traveled from Vietnam to England, much
of the way in mortal danger, could not "get off their
butts" was just a bit more than I could stomach.

360

ocean

Troubled or still, water is always water. What difference can embodiment or disembodiment make to the liberated? Whether calm or stormy, the sameness of the ocean suffers no change.

YOGAVASISTHA

duty calls

Yukiko and Midoli appeared one evening with a small, skinny, pale-faced Asian girl who, they told me, was a Vietnamese called Nga. I thought I knew all the local Boat People, at least by sight, but Nga was new to me.

"She's very bright," said Yukiko.

"I'm sure she is."

"Yes, in Vietnam she was a PhD student."

"Good for her."

"She needs to learn English. I said you would teach her."

"You did what? I already help out a whole family of ten Boat People. I don't have time."

"It would only be one hour a week. She's a very quick learner. And she's a Buddhist."

"So? They're all Buddhists!"

"Then it's your duty to help. So that's settled. Can she have her first lesson now? Good, we'll come back later. Bye!"

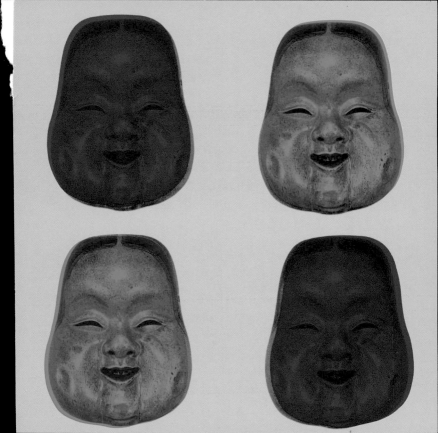

the way of the sword

People assume that Japanese girls learn things like flower arranging, the tea ceremony, or perhaps, calligraphy. One evening Midoli and Yukiko were making their way through Cambridge when some local low-lifes started to give them a hard time. They ignored them at first but then the sidewalk was blocked and it seemed time to get assertive. Yukiko had borrowed my golfing umbrella and, stepping in front of her friend, went into the kendo "on guard" position. There were hoots of derision from the lads and one of them, most unwisely, made a grab for the brolly. Whack! It took a couple more whacks before they got the message that this five-foot girl meant business. Midoli was astonished, and so was I when I got my umbrella back. Yukiko had never once mentioned that she studied kendo. However, in best samurai tradition, she did give her "sword" a name. She called it Boy Beater.

363
worry juice

One night I had so much on my mind that I tossed and turned and just couldn't get to sleep. I worried and worried and worried. Then, to my amazement, the clouds cleared and I felt fine. By about 3 A.M. I'd worried so much that I seemed to have run out of worry juice. Which made me think. If my worries could so suddenly cease, then they hadn't been real in the first place.

what happened?

For those who like neat endings, this is what happened. Lek still lives in the same house and teaches at the same school in Bangkok, where she is now Head of English. Her daughters are all grown up. Little Monkey, who now goes by her regular name, which I'm not allowed to reveal, is an air hostess for Thai International. The Old Lady lived to an immense age before dying in her sleep and leaving the school to her children. Sean now lives in London where he works as a teacher and is actively involved in various Buddhist projects. James got a job with the British Council and occasionally e-mails from the Middle East. Yukiko went back to Japan but was too Westernized for any Japanese man to marry, which was definitely their loss. She has a university job and describes herself as a "happy, ink-stained perpetual student." She still sees Midoli, who is married and has two children.

the last word

Much speech leads to silence. Better to hold fast to the void.

TAO TE CHING

Published by MQ Publications Limited
12 The Ivories, 6–8 Northampton Street
London N1 2HY
Tel: 020 7359 2244   Fax: 020 7359 1616
email: mail@mqpublications.com

Copyright © MQ Publications Limited 2003

TEXT © Robert Allen 2003
ILLUSTRATIONS danny@dogtag.uk.com
DESIGN balley design associates

ISBN: 1-84072-428-5

5 7 9 0 8 6 4

Printed and bound in China